A
KARMIC
ADVENTURE

Liz Hayes and Rhea Gargour

A KARMIC ADVENTURE

© 2024 by Liz Hayes & Rhea Gargour. All rights reserved.
Editor: Tommy Crabtree

No part of this book may be used or reproduced in any matter whatsoever without written permission. For information please contact:

WE ARE KMB LTD
63-66 Hatton Garden
London, EC1N 8LE

ISBN number paperback: 978-1-7393783-7-0
ISBN number ebook: 978-1-7393783-6-3

Table of Contents

Introduction
Champagne Supernova — 13

Chapter One
7 — 19
Back At One — 24

Chapter Two
9 to 5 — 29
L-O-V-E — 31

Chapter Three
C'est la Vie — 35
That's Life — 39

Chapter Four
Thinking 'Bout Love — 45
Think Twice — 48

Chapter Five
Do Wot You Do — 53
Freedom — 56

Chapter Six
Eternal Flame — 61
Time After Time — 65

Chapter Seven
One Way Or Another — 71
Don't You (Forget About Me) — 75

Chapter Eight
  The Next Episode   79
  Blaze Of Glory   82

Chapter Nine
  Knowing Me, Knowing You   87
  Pandora's Box   92

Chapter Ten
  Show Me Love   97
  Don't Worry Baby   99

Chapter Eleven
  Hold the Line   105
  Take It On the Run   107

Chapter Twelve
  For What It's Worth   111
  My Way   114

Chapter Thirteen
  Heaven Must Have Sent You   117
  Heaven Help   121

Chapter Fourteen
  Good Vibrations   127
  Come Home To Me   130

Chapter Fifteen
  You're Not Alone   135
  Beyond The Invisible   138

Chapter Sixteen
  How Will I Know   143
  Can You Feel It   147

Chapter Seventeen
  Another One Bites The Dust 151
  All Right Now 156

Chapter Eighteen
  Body Language 161
  All Of Me 166

Chapter Nineteen
  Against All Odds 171
  Something Happened On The Way To Heaven 174

Chapter Twenty
  Hand In My Pocket 181
  A Million Love Songs 185

Chapter Twenty-One
  Dark Side Of The Moon 189
  The Other Side Of Life 194

Chapter Twenty-Two
  I've Got You Under My Skin 199
  Nothing's Gonna Stop Us Now 201

Chapter Twenty-Three
  Who Are You? 205
  Won't Get Fooled Again 207

Chapter Twenty-Four
  Love & Hate 213
  The Voice Within 215

Chapter Twenty-Five
  Take Me To Church 221
  Church Of The Poison Mind 224

Chapter Twenty-Six
  Never Can Say Goodbye   229
  Follow The Sun   232

Chapter Twenty-Seven
  Are You Gonna Go My Way?   237
  I Wanna Dance with Somebody   240

Chapter Twenty-Eight
  Stop Crying Your Heart Out   245
  Stand By Me   248

Chapter Twenty-Nine
  Redemption Song   253
  Always On The Run   256

Chapter Thirty
  What's Up?   261
  You Wish   264

Chapter Thirty-One
  Perfect   269
  Sweetheart   273

Chapter Thirty-Two
  The Way We Were   277
  What's Love Got To Do With It?   281

Chapter Thirty-Three
  Walk This Way   285
  Send Me An Angel   288

Chapter Thirty-Four
  All For Love   293
  That Thing You Do   296

Chapter Thirty-Five
  Starman   301
  Just Like Heaven   306

Chapter Thirty-Six
  Love Is A Beautiful Thing   311
  Love Story   313

Conclusion
  The Edge Of Heaven   319

About KMB   329

Acknowledgments   331

*"We can easily forgive a child who is afraid of the dark;
the real tragedy of life is when men
are afraid of the light."*

—**Plato**

Champagne Supernova
Rhea

Most uplifting or inspiring stories include an uncomfortable beginning. Whether it is the couch potato who gets off the couch to win the marathon, the unemployed genius who discovers their dream job, or the loveless loner who rides off into the sunset with their perfect match, the story always starts with the person that they were, and through the adventure of the story, they finally overcome themselves to become the person they were always meant to be… and get the thing they always wanted.

As I'm writing the introduction, one might assume (as I did) that I would follow the same format, especially since in every book, all I do is talk about myself and how I changed. But that would make me just like everyone else, make this book just like every other book, and make my story just like every other story. And we know by now I am not here to be like everyone else.

Don't get me wrong; I do often wonder how I got here—to have become the person who has written a bunch of books, who records a podcast with a gifted spiritual medium (as you will read, I have met quite a few), who finds the beauty and joy in everything, who operates from a place of Love rather than fear and ego, and the one who is truly happy.

But then I remember that's who I started as. I was the child who heard the beat of my little heart and knew that it connected me to something so much greater. I had ideas about how one could move within time and how a mini ceremony with plants and flowers from my garden could make the sun come out. I believed in Love because I *was* Love, and experiencing that Love was a pleasure.

Then people called me crazy, fanciful, and just plain delusional. I was told that the only things that were real were those we could see and touch. And I believed them. I was shamed into focusing on what made sense, how $x + y = z$, and that logic was king. Piece by piece, I took all those beliefs and hid them away, afraid that I would be judged for them.

Slowly, I shut off my emotional connection to be cool like everyone else, shut off my spiritual connection that told me everything would work out, and developed such a high level of body dysmorphia that I stopped seeing who I was. Piece by piece, I took that happiness and hid it away.

I stopped sharing my feelings and trusting everyone, including myself. I may have still wanted Love, but I bought into the lie that it was earned and sacrificed for and that relationships had to fit a certain mold to be successful. I lost myself to the rules of how life needed to be and how I needed to comply with them. I used other people as a barometer of my worth, and even though I wanted connection, I never connected to anyone properly.

Piece by piece, I took that light and those yummy feelings and hid them away.

Then I was left with a bigger problem: I was fucking miserable.

I pretended to everyone else that I wasn't (because when you slowly diminish yourself for other people, the only thing that matters is what others think), but secretly, I was empty. I looked to everyone else and everything else to save me (again, if you kill yourself off for others, then they are the only ones who can bring you back to life), but I also wondered what they were saving me from (myself, perhaps?).

For those who haven't read the prior books, my life began to change when I'd finally had enough and said, "Fuck This." I was done seeking validation from others, expecting the other shoe to drop, and plastering on a smile whilst bracing for impact. I wanted more from my life, and even though I didn't know what that looked like, anything was better than what I was settling for.

That "Fuck This" led to many more, where I had to face every piece of my separated self and put them back together. I met mirror after mirror that showed me my pain, my shadow, and my core fear—how I believed I wasn't *good enough* to change my life for the better. But the more I listened to my heart, the more I remembered that I had always been *good enough*, and things got *better enough* for me to want more for my life.

Once we go through our entire karmic undoing process and we realize nothing is holding us back, it gets interesting. We have all the freedom that we've always wished for to make our lives what we want them to be, but we may not know how to make it happen.

In *A Karmic Attraction*, I talked about how I learnt to listen to my heart, and in *A Karmic Affair*, I understood what Love really was. In this, the final book of the series, I share how they came together to create the life that I desired. All the wisdom and determination I gleaned could be applied to my life so that I could navigate my new world from my heart, rather than from my fears and ego.

All those people who we "were," all those iterations of ourselves that we are constantly trying to outrun, over-explain, or hide—they aren't different people at all. They are us. But in separating ourselves from who we believe we used to be, we aren't just ignoring parts of ourselves, we are often ignoring the parts that make us enchanted.

Those parts of us that make us different, hopeful, or loving aren't shameful; they are the key to our power. That's why we cannot override them or pretend they never existed. They share the responsibility of creating the world that we know to be possible, and they are the reason that we can be more than we are today.

Every step we take doesn't replace who we used to be but stretches us beyond our perceived limitations so that we can see we are capable of so much more—and thus experience so much more. We aren't getting rewarded for our transformation or being grateful to some higher being who has given us three wishes. We are merely remembering who we always have been.

This book isn't a story about how we rise from the ashes, turn into fancy butterflies, and fly off into the wind, creating our dreams as we go. Nor is it about how we change into someone new. It's the story of how we remember ourselves and what happens once we do. We have always been perfect, we've just forgotten it piece by piece.

Thank God I remembered.

7
Liz

Karma is a gift. It was always intended as a gift, but it's been misunderstood and regarded as punishment. As the saying goes, "What goes around comes around" or "You reap what you sow." We are taught that whatever we do will come back to us, and we therefore need to carefully consider everything we say or do. As a result, the notion of karma has been used to make us fearful and to control our behavior. But fear removes our control, and that is the opposite of karma. We are not here to drown in our Shit, choke on our fears, and feed our egos. Rather, we are here to transcend them all and live in a place of our own making.

Karma is the new/old game—new because we're finally able to see karma for what it is, the gift that keeps on giving until we're finished with it, and old, well, because it's been around for longer than millennia. In this new version of this old game, we're here to end our karma once and for all.

Karma reminds us that we are in the driver's seat of our lives. We are not victims, nor are we mere passengers on someone else's journey. Rather, we are the agents of our lives. Karma tells us that we have always been, but it's just that we've forgotten that somewhere along the way in leading lives of Separation (aka Third-dimensional consciousness, aka 3D).

Separation, or the belief that we are not connected to anything else, is underpinned by polarity. This polarity informs the rules that govern our lives, how we live, and how the tentpoles of 3D consciousness (religion, government, and economic systems) function. For every right, there is a wrong; for every virtue, there is a vice. Black opposes white, and good balances out bad. As a society, we tread along this narrow spectrum, judging and criticizing ourselves and others if we fail to stay in our lane and live the "right" kind of life, maintain the "right" job, attend the "right" schools, and demonstrate "good" behavior and "proper" demeanor. Any failure to live up to these arbitrary rules makes us outliers and outcasts, deemed unfit for society and unworthy.

We've been unwinding from 3D Separation consciousness as we've prepared ourselves for the leap into Oneness (aka Fifth-dimensional consciousness, aka 5D). One way or another, we've had Separation thrown into our faces, and we've been forced to confront all the ways in which we've hurt and damaged ourselves by living in and propping it up.

For anyone who is curious, there is a fourth dimension, but there is little reason to address it since it has nothing to do with our rise in consciousness. 4D is the place of archetypes and paradigms. We cannot remain in that space for long because if you imagine these dimensions as sine waves, 4D is at the bottom of the wave and is very brief. We don't necessarily pass through it as much as we hop over on our way to further our consciousness.

Once we understand that our lives are the result of our perceived limited choices, we see that we can make different choices and create a life of our own making, one where peace and happiness are truly possible. That is what this lifetime is about, and that is what we are here for—to kill our karma and get ourselves into Oneness consciousness or, quite simply, to a place of peace in our lives where we don't look to cancel, weaken, or disempower others.

That's always been the goal of 3D: to focus on self-punishment, self-immolation, and self-blame so that we can't see that we're always playing a losing game. That game has only one objective in mind: to ensure that we are never, nor could we ever, find a way to self-empowerment and self-determination. In this way, we are always going to remain dependent on someone or something else to maintain our survival. And so long as we remain dependent, weak individuals, we will never realize what we are capable of.

After all the time we've spent in Separation—disconnected from our true nature, which is perfect and not separate—we've needed something like karma to jolt us awake because we wouldn't pay attention. Karma is the whole package wrapped in a bow. It allows us to encapsulate our core fear (*I Am not Good Enough*) that keeps us in Separation and gives us a way to burn it out.

It does so through a series of growth opportunities and lessons that remind us that we truly are *good enough*, which life in Separation made us forget.

Until now, I've used various words to describe karma and its principles without fully defining what karma is. Any previous attempt to explain it falls short because karma cannot be fully understood while it is defining our lives (a bit like identifying the crux of a problem when we're in the midst of a drama). We can only really grasp it when we are no longer in its grasp, both individually and collectively.

Karma is power. It is the purest form of power we have outside of divine power. It exists for two reasons:

1. To exercise our divine will to ensure we are never far from divine consciousness; and
2. To keep us from falling prey to our fallibilities when we are not living in full divine identity—which is why it has been long misunderstood as the thing that comes back to torture us. It's not for fun, rather it always points out when we are not our full divine selves.

Once we burn through all that keeps us apart from the Divine, we no longer require it to serve our consciousness. Rather, through the karmic undoing process and by living our fullest fate, that power is transcended, and we can live fully as the Divine.

Karma gives us a framework through which we can experience our core fear. These karmic stories allow us to confront the ways we've incorporated Separation into our lives without completely imploding in the process. In case you aren't caught up, the seven themes are:

1. I Am Unlovable: I cannot be loved as I am.
2. I Am Undeserving: No one will accept me for who I choose to be.
3. I Am not Worthy: Who I am is not *good enough* in anyone else's eyes.
4. I Am Imperfect: I will never be *good enough*, so I will hide who I am.
5. I Am Nothing: I am not strong enough to be able to shift my current reality to another one.
6. I Am Evil: There isn't enough light to illuminate my presence.
7. I Am Broken: I do not have enough power to be who I am.

Back At One

These karmic themes encompass the core fear of *I Am not Good Enough* that will always provide the roadmap to heal our Shit, burn out our fear, and rid ourselves of our egos, which keep us in Separation.

The ego requires us to exist within the bounds of our fear. It's what keeps us safe in Separation. To live in Separation, we require something to keep us in our lane and assure us that we're right, even though nothing about Separation feels natural. The ego allows us to lie to ourselves, to make our fears seem smaller than they are, and it leads us to believe that by having the right kind of persona, we won't be left exposed.

We're never free from Separation until we're free from our egos, which we can only be when we eliminate judgment. The ego tells us not to fuck things up by sending that message we're desperate to send or reminds us that we may not deserve the future we so desperately want because we made mistakes in the past. It keeps us and others in line, killing any sense of hope by creating expectations that will never be met.

The ego can be cruel, but only because life as we know it is cruel and unforgiving. We've played through this story lifetime after lifetime. We've become used to and are practically pros at living in Separation; so for karma to wake us up and remind us that we've been living a lie, and that Separation is not the only way to live, is some nuclear-level kind of shit.

That's why Rhea loves to call karma "the Shit that Happens." It's the result of life in 3D Separation. We've been somnolent through our waking days while lying awake at night, wondering what the fuck is wrong with us. We've been self-medicating, trying to numb the pain, and dabbling in every coping mechanism from meditation to plant medicine, from anti-depressants to alcohol and whatever other legal or illegal means enable us to forget how much we are suffering.

So we opt for the devil we know instead of the devil we don't. Our egos have calculated which is the devil we can tolerate. But by perpetuating Separation, the ego has perpetuated our pain, which is why we can no longer live with it. To kill our egos, we need to eliminate judgment from our lives. In place of judgment, we need acceptance, and acceptance happens when we enable compassion. That's when the seemingly impossible task of burning out that falsehood, *I Am not Good Enough*, becomes possible.

From our personal to professional relationships, as well as our relationship with ourselves and the outside world, our Shit gets thrown up and rubbed in our faces. While everything with karma is relational in that we play out our karmic stories with one another, it has everything to do with *our* perspective. It is this perspective that has informed our human experiences, making them incredibly disappointing and impressively unimpressive.

When we are in our karma, we are locked in our core fear that we are not *good enough*, and our lives are set up in such a way to reinforce that belief, underscored by a particular karmic theme—unlovable, not worthy, undeserving, imperfect, broken, evil, and nothing—which plays out through our karmic story. As we resolve each issue that crops up during our karmic stories and lean into our fears to burn them out, we come closer to finding peace and wholeness within.

As we do this, we discover that not only are we pretty amazing beings, but so is everyone else because often what makes them annoying assholes is that they're battling their own karma too. That's when we can shed our egos since we no longer need to hold the idea of Separation outside of ourselves. When we can live without judgment and our ego, we are well on our way to experiencing what happiness really means.

There's just one catch: when there are no rules, anything is possible, and when anything is possible, everything is possible. It doesn't make for a lawless life or even a reckless one; rather, it allows us to come into our power by deciding for ourselves what our own values are and to develop standards by which we choose to live as opposed to those established by others. So, the more empowered we become in choosing our lives for ourselves, the more those values and standards reflect our self-respect, compassion, and authentic self.

Karmic challenges force us to grow and gather the scattered pieces of ourselves to come into wholeness and our power. It isn't easy, especially since the tentpoles that uphold Separation have to come down. As a result, we're undergoing a massive transformation from the inside out, witnessing our entire lives as we've known them—along with our entire world—come undone.

5D challenges, on the other hand, are in place to help us expand our wisdom, broaden our sense of self, and further cement our divine identities. By allowing ourselves to live in the present, we come to understand that the lessons to be gained from these challenges contribute to a greater joy we bring to our experiences.

That is the power of karma and what makes it such a special gift. That is why we teach that karma is never *a* bitch. It's meant to be *our* bitch. This is the lifetime to end our karmic stories for good. Once we end it, we can realize our true nature, which is divine and whole.

9 to 5
Rhea

For a long time, I thought that suffering was normal, or if it wasn't, then the problem was with me. I was in a job that I was told was the "right" profession so that I could live the "right" way and grow up in the "right" direction. I had to follow the rules, and if I couldn't hack it, then I wasn't trying hard enough and I wasn't *good enough*.

But I hated feeling not *good enough*, so much so that I did everything I could to not feel alive. I ate and smoked a lot, and I dabbled in New Age whatever—looking for the shortcuts and the answers to how I could find joy—whilst wondering why anyone would keep going when the payoff never came.

The dissonance between doing what I thought I should do and what I wanted bled into every part of my life—whether it was panic attacks at dinner, sleepless Sunday nights, or lashing out whenever I felt like exploding. My issue wasn't my career trajectory, the amount of money that I was earning, or the fact that I had to wake up far too early for my taste. The issue was that I wasn't doing it for me. I was doing it so that I could fit into a specific box that I had convinced myself was emblematic of who I needed to be.

That box wasn't something that I created, it was something that I'd adopted so that I could label myself in a way that others would find commendable. But in making my career choices based on others' opinions, I also made them responsible when it made me unhappy. Liz's iconic phrase in *A Karmic Affair*, "I did it for you," echoed in my head every time I swiped that entry card and took the lift to the seventh floor to my desk. I didn't want anyone to be embarrassed by me, not understand me, or walk slowly backwards every time I mentioned my work. I wanted to be a known quantity so that I could easily assimilate into whatever conversation I was having.

There are certain attributes that separate us from the person next to us, and they fall into three main categories: career, social position, and relationship status. In fact, we have created hierarchies in every facet of our lives, and we work to ensure that we reach the highest level possible or accept our status within the hierarchy, whilst lamenting that we wish we could do something different and making excuses as to why we can't. We cover up all the Shit we don't feel we have the bandwidth to deal with whilst telling ourselves that if we had to face it, we wouldn't even know how to deal with it. But that is what keeps 3D alive: our feelings of powerlessness and our inability to face our issues.

I kept myself stuck in a minefield of limiting beliefs and expectations. I readily took every shortcut, bypass, and way to miss out on the work. But I didn't go down the "right" road just for my own self-satisfaction, it was an inspired form of people-pleasing. Except, really, I was serving myself. Problem was, in trying to make the best of a painful situation, I inadvertently made things a hell of a lot worse. I filled my body with resentment whilst trying to catch my breath. And the more I did so, the more I gave my power away until I believed I had none left other than what someone else could bestow upon me.

I may have wanted to be "right," but this clearly wasn't the way I was going to get there. I had to untangle the root of the issue. Otherwise, I would be looking to everyone else to save me and cycling through my powerlessness every time my expectations remained unfulfilled.

L-O-V-E

When none of my expectations were fulfilled, regardless of how hard I worked to prove that I was worthy of them, I couldn't keep going. I also couldn't outrun the voice that kept asking me what the point was. I thought that to ensure my survival was to accept that everything was pointless—to either accept that joyful work was a pipedream or to eschew financial success and be unhappy in another way. I assumed that I'd always be stuck in a tradeoff, compromise, or catch-22. But I didn't want to live simply to survive, or for the ticking of the clock to be a relief as it marched me closer to the end of pointlessness. For me, the solution would be not to live at all.

This was my first spiritual reckoning. There were many more to come as time went on, but in many ways, that was the darkest of them all because it was the loudest and lasted the longest. But it also had to be because, at that moment, I was the most separated from the point of my life and all the parts of myself—all the while telling myself that this was what it meant to be a grown-up.

Looking back, it makes perfect sense why everything happened. My issue wasn't about fitting into a world that already existed, it was about creating my own. It was never about a revolution where I was fighting someone else, it was really a revolution where I was fighting my demons. It was never about trying to make 3D work for me, it was about leaving it behind for good. My question "What's the point?" was a call to action: to find out what was the point for me. Otherwise, I would forever be running scared of the next uncontrollable situation, the next panic attack, and the next meltdown. The ego is truly a bitch.

I knew that I needed to find a reason for life that wasn't just about surviving because being like everyone else wasn't working for me. Intuitively, I knew that reason involved joy because whenever I experienced it, I felt more like myself. But I felt so far removed from all the possibilities that seemed to come with joy that I couldn't figure out how to get there.

Eventually, the answer came through my guardian angel (my maternal grandmother) whilst I was crying in her kitchen, fed up and tired of asking the same question without finding an answer. She turned to me and said, "For me, the point is Love."

It was at that moment I knew it to be true for me, too. Love was such a key component of why I was in body. Even though the answer came from her lips, the answer also came from inside of me just as loudly. I felt the calmness of my emotional body, the peace in my physical one, the agreement in my mental one, and the knowing in my spiritual one. It was clear because it was a moment of wholeness, where all my bodies were so perfectly aligned that they could all agree on it. My first point was Love.

Even though I knew that my first point was Love, I wasn't sure how to apply it. I didn't even know what Love really was. As relayed in *A Karmic Affair,* my approaches to romantic relationships were confused and informed by societal expectations that had distorted Love to the point that it wasn't Love at all. I thought someone else's presence in my life was a measure of my success, I thought I had to play toxic games to get them, and I thought that my life could only start when I found my "other half." So, until that happened, I focused on other people's relationships instead.

It was easy for me to start working in the field of domestic violence. It was relationship-focused and tapped into another part of me that I felt was here to help others. If I couldn't bring justice to a world worrying about mergers and insurance claims, then I needed to bring justice to a world where relationships were being exploited. And there were bonus points too. It still was a palatable career choice—especially when we successfully campaigned to make coercive control a crime in the UK.

Sure, I had to deal with lots of people asking me if I was going to burn my bra, making jokes about how their wives abused them by asking them to do the dishes, and my dates becoming a little awkward when the subject of my job came up. But I was making a difference that wasn't hurting me in the process. I had experienced joy when it came to my work, even for a moment, and therefore I knew that it was possible.

It wasn't helping me, though. I was still trying to control what I did so I could control what happened next and how I was perceived. I applied outdated ideas of how work should be whilst simultaneously eschewing any type of conventional labels because I didn't want to feel trapped again. I put all my value in my job, defined myself by my achievements, and excused walking away from corporate life by evidencing the people I helped and the law that I had helped create. I turned my career into an identity, and I used it to justify all the pain that preceded it. In fact, even when I left and started my own business, the same thing happened again—I wondered why, even though I was doing something that brought me joy, I still felt split.

C'est la Vie
Liz

Our power is an extension of our free will. It's the ability to do and act as we wish, whenever we wish. This power is contingent upon our freedom. The greater our freedom to exercise our free will, the more powerful we are. This experience is critical to the 3D experiment. We cannot know the full extent of our capacity to create and destroy if we cannot exercise it to the limit.

Yet, we cannot understand where those limits lie if we do not push ourselves to learn what they are. Furthermore, we cannot grasp exactly what we are capable of if we do not allow ourselves to grow through adversity. Except the more we become ruled by 3D and the ego rules judgment, the less of our divine selves we can experience (because the soul can only be separate from the Divine for so long). The less able we are to operate from our divine selves, the less power we have because we no longer have the freedom to exercise our free will.

We've been taught to suck it up. We've been sold the notion that while life could be better, it could be a helluva lot worse. "Life sucks and then you die," "Be happy you're alive," "Be grateful you didn't end up like *that* person," or "You get what you get, and you don't get upset" are pithy platitudes intended to help us wade through our shitty lives.

While they can certainly console us on the worst of days, the truth is, they don't make life as we know it particularly appealing. As a matter of fact, we have to wonder why we would use such bathroom-stall philosophy as a guiding force for our lives, especially when they don't actually change our circumstances. Recognizing that things could be worse really doesn't inspire meaningful change, it just gets us to accept our shitty conditions.

Of course, acceptance can help shift our perspectives enough to allow us to appreciate all the "good" things in life, but it doesn't empower us to consider what we could do to make it better. All it really takes is to face that life really does suck. Separation sucks. Not being at one with the Divine sucks. Feeling impotent in life sucks the big one. But until we really acknowledge it, look it in the eye, stare it down, wrestle with it, and consider how true it really is, we won't make it better.

Even though we have karma to thank for our loops of disempowerment, it's important to consider why we so easily fall prey to victimhood. The reason goes beyond our core fear, insecurities, and imperfections. It also lies beyond our perceptions of our divinity and lands squarely at the feet of our collective human history.

This history is full of winners and losers, conquerors and the conquered, colonizers and the colonized, kings and serfs, as well as tyrants and subjects. While this hierarchy can be attributed to 3D consciousness, which is underscored by polarity, there is a nuanced perspective that needs to be addressed to understand why we are contending with an aspect of Otherness that often becomes equated with Separation consciousness but isn't the same at all. It is an understanding that needs to be illuminated to grasp that even when we burn out our karma and release some of our ego, there's a part of us that may continue to doomscroll through our social media or react to every asinine tweet that pops up every two seconds.

We are like young children who need attention from their parents to show what we've learned and receive approval or validation in return. Yet, the problem is that in constantly waiting for and needing approval, the opportunity for learning and growth becomes stunted because we've tied our identity to what others think of us or how we are received by them.

When our sense of self becomes dependent upon external validation, we cannot possibly live from an empowered place. On the contrary, we perpetuate our disempowerment, which keeps us stuck in a game of our own making.

One by one, our freedoms are being eroded, not for the sake of Oneness as some may perceive, but for the sake of Separation. The greater the chasms of Separation, the more they threaten to swallow us when we are not in our power to stop it. These chasms get bigger when there are more people available to feed Separation, and they feed it not out of fear but out of misplaced empathy.

As contrarian as it sounds, there is no place for empathy in Oneness because it requires recognizing that someone is weak or not in their power. It gives the illusion that someone cannot step into their power on their own. This is not to say that we cannot give or receive help. Rather, when we presume that someone is incapable of coming into their power on their own *and* that we must be the one to empower them, we perpetuate their disempowerment while fueling our own power under the guise of being a good Samaritan.

In 3D, this could work to an extent. Hierarchical structures allow for the top-to-bottom approach. However, in 5D Oneness, which is more of a horizontal model, it does not work. Holding onto the belief that people are helpless and incapable maintains Separation consciousness and demands people continually support it out of some misguided virtue. The longer we hold on to this belief system, the longer we remain locked into these systems that demand more of our power in return. This is anathema to our souls who not only need to be free to create and operate from their full divine power but who did not come here to be hobbled and disabled by outdated systems that do little to actually aid citizens when their sole purpose is to merely maintain Separation.

It hasn't been easy. Still, many are inclined to fall back into their victimhood. Those who remain at the head of the 3D tentpoles take advantage of people's Separation by selling them their disempowerment, hustling to keep their positions of power by propping up others' weaknesses and fallibilities as virtuous reasons to slow others' progress and evolution. Rather than push for growth and consciousness, which would benefit everyone, their approach is to disable it by discouraging creativity and by curbing individual speech and personal power.

It's the game of power. To keep the systems humming along, those who maintain the hierarchy do so as a way to maintain their own power within the system, thereby creating a symbiotic relationship where power is sourced through someone else, not the individual. In turn, the more these tentpoles sap individuals of their own power, the less power they have for themselves because the hierarchy of these systems ensures no one will ever have more than those at the very top.

That's Life

Our past lifetimes aren't always intertwined with our karma. They can also leave a traumatic piece for us to deal with and end up manifesting through a variety of relationships, not to mention leave us feeling so karmic that they color our experiences in our daily lives. They especially occur in matters of the heart and play out in our closest or most intimate relationships, such as romantic or familial ties. These past life experiences often hook us to the relationship or struggle for longer than would serve us, but we're often so blinded by a strong need to "fix" something that is not fixable, at least not in this lifetime—or we surrender before we've given ourselves a chance.

We have spent our lives, many lifetimes for that matter, trying to get our power back only to be pushed into a corner and suffering the consequences for our attempts. Time and again we have been shown that despite our best efforts, we will never fully defeat those at the top of the tentpoles—those with more money, more influence, and more god-fearing devotion. We could never *be enough* for ourselves.

Fuck if it isn't frustrating to live in a cycle of our own demise and powerlessness; to know our perfection deep down or have had a taste of pure joy and ecstasy, only to tell ourselves it can't be that way all the time—to have to direct our focus to the everyday bullshit and reckless order of our lives, that we never created for ourselves in the first place yet find ourselves fighting through all the time.

As if that weren't enough, to keep believing it can't be any other way is the rock bottom of our powerlessness. But that's how it is because it's been the ethos of many generations. That we didn't start the fire, and therefore can't even put it out or keep kicking the proverbial can down the rocky road of life, is just a way in which we justify staying wherever we are.

The fucked-up thing, however, is that throughout all of this, there has been a constant, which is God. Not just the God in the sky or the gods of war and seasons and whatever, but a God who has been looked to throughout time. So even when we have found ourselves on the losing end of this power game, we all look to the same source of life and death and wonder: "What the actual fuck is going on here?"

Even those at the top of the tentpoles look to God or have used God to further a cause. In God We Trust. (Consider that the one at the top of the religion tentpoles often wields the greatest influence because of their divine connection.) Often, we cannot remove God from any of our equations, really. The same goes for the devil. But reconciling this is almost impossible when we consider the horrific atrocities and crimes committed throughout human history.

We've asked these questions time and again, often without getting a single satisfying answer. Why do "bad" things happen to "good" people? How can God allow something like this to happen? And since God couldn't possibly allow for something "bad" to happen, then it must be some work of the devil, or it's a "mystery." You know, because God works in "mysterious" ways. But there's no mystery, there's never been a mystery, except why we can't see the bigger picture, which has been Separation all along.

When we cannot be in our fullest power, our ability to create and destroy becomes distorted as our egos manipulate it to mitigate our fears. Values become attributed to our actions, hierarchies become established, and Otherness moves from minor distinctions to even wider differences. Our power no longer depends on what we perceive it to be and our personal experience of it but becomes wholly relational, making our concepts of power conditional on others. To have more power means someone has to have less.

This is hardly an argument for communism or some perceived equalizing system. No one can be fully empowered if they depend upon another to give them power. This merely perpetuates Separation and feeds the systems of influence and power that prop up 3D. Yet, when we are in Oneness, we can all see one another for all that we are: the Divine in action. When we are in our most divine power, there isn't anything we wouldn't do to help others realize their own divinity. But we can only do that by seeing the Divine in them.

Divine power belongs wholly and utterly to the individual first and foremost. It can only be sourced through the individual, which comes from within. That is, the more divine consciousness they hold (as in, they are the Divine), the more powerful they are. When they can enter into this consciousness, they can then express it fully and share it with others who are also divinely sourced. To do this demands three things of us:

1. Freedom.

The more freedom we have, the more we can live unencumbered by the demands, expectations, and rules that have been set by others. Even if we internalize these standards and make them our own, realizing our freedom means we can choose how to live our lives. It is and has always been up to us.

2. Determination.

We can only know what we are capable of when we pursue what we most desire. Coming out of Separation through our karma requires a kind of fortitude that many of us no longer have because we've internalized the belief that we are not capable.

3. Responsibility.

To understand our divine power is to accept that we have designed our lives as they are. When we accept this responsibility for our lives, we can take ownership of all that's happened in our lives up until now. This does not mean we are to blame for everything. There is a difference between accountability and blame. Blame reinforces our disempowerment. Accountability acknowledges we've had a hand in creating our lives; it also accepts that while we may not foresee the outcome because of our egos or karma, what happened has happened. There is no changing anything once it becomes a part of our past. All that we can ever do is move forward and learn from the lessons that come our way.

Thinking 'Bout Love
Rhea

Every time I ticked another accomplishment off the list but circled back to myself and found that person unchanged, I went looking again to find someone else to help. And every time I questioned whether the work was enough, I was also faced with the fear that I wouldn't be enough without it.

That is why purpose in 3D is so fucked up—we pin our worth on literally achieving the impossible. We can't fix someone else, no matter how much we wish we could. We can't even fix ourselves. Sure, we change a job, change a process, or even change a law, but we cannot give someone else the power that they have given away. All we can do is put salve on the wound to stop it bleeding, but they could still pick the scab right off the second we turn our backs or, failing that, not even see that we've handed them a bandage. That means we can create the conditions for freedom, but unless the other person chooses it, it is merely words on paper.

We are the most powerful beings in our world, and how we feel about the world entirely relates to how we feel about ourselves. But we take our actions too seriously, and we base our future on our perceived present—partly because we don't want to choose how to spend our time in this life, but mostly because we value our reputation and image rather than our joy.

Labeling others based on superficial differences is ineffective, and measuring them according to the standards we have decided is equally flawed. We make everyone else God whilst still hoping that we are god-like (or maybe god-adjacent) by emulating them. This not only ensures that we remain within the box that stifles us, but we also bring everyone else into it, leaving no oxygen for anyone to breathe.

We can't outsource our power to someone else, be it personal or societal, as we are putting responsibility onto someone or something else that cannot take it. When we ask someone else to save us, or we measure our worth by how we have saved them, we are putting a responsibility on them that does not belong. We not only limit our potential, we limit theirs, too, as no one can be free to wield their power, even if it is in expectation, assumption, or coercion alone.

If we rely on other people's reactions to us to determine whether we are successful or worthy, we limit our potential and the choices that we allow ourselves to make. But when we can find ourselves again, we not only change our worlds but also change them for the people around us. On a micro level, we are more pleasant to be around, so everyone has a better time, but as we allow ourselves to get bigger and spread our light past our intimate relationships, we inspire others to spread their light, too.

My achievements are a testament to how hard I worked, how much I wanted to change someone's world, and how much I needed a purpose to feel alive. But they are also a testament to how far my ego will go to protect me. That's why, when each goal was satisfied, I didn't feel satisfied with them. I felt lost, and I searched for the next achievement in lieu of searching for myself.

To truly grow up, we must kill the ego. We can't be powerful when we limit that power to what we believe our lives should look like and how we identify ourselves. We are letting something outside of us dictate how our power should manifest, which isn't power at all. The more we push ourselves into a prescribed box (which feels more like a coffin with every word I write), the more we also prevent ourselves from bringing those perfectly unique gifts into our world. We also don't allow for innovation or to see how powerful we really are.

Without taking ownership of my life, I was sullying my integrity, making my work into a results-based endeavor rather than an empowerment one. My issue was that I thought that helping others was why I was joyful, but it was actually the other way around. By engaging in something that brought me joy, the byproduct was that I helped others. How I felt was the catalyst for what happened outside of me, and in engaging with those feelings, I changed my world and helped others change theirs.

It's important to see that at our core, we are exactly who we need to be, and that person is perfectly gifted—flaws and all. Part of being a grown-up is giving others space to do the same. When we can do it for ourselves, we can also do it for each other so that the 3D that we end within, which is replaced by something far more beautiful, can expand exponentially.

The new world comes from within us instead of being imposed on us by someone else. That's the true revolution. We first serve ourselves by healing our Shit, and it's then, with our whole healed selves, that we can look outside of our own myopic view and figure out how to serve the collective.

Think Twice

We have been pitted against each other whilst being told we need each other to survive. The individual must sacrifice themselves for the collective (be it a collective of two or two billion) and must also do it better than everyone else. That's why everything we do is measured through someone else's eyes but also why FOMO (fear of missing out) isn't just a snazzy term but a pandemic where no one ever feels like they have enough because they are secretly worried that they aren't *good enough*.

No wonder we are all busting our asses to be perfect whilst worrying that the person next to us is perfect. No wonder we view relationships as responsibility for the other person's happiness rather than a mutually shared joy. No wonder we think that the harder we work, the more success we earn. No wonder we think that to be divine, we must sacrifice everything we have. We have been taught that this is the only way to be, and we then perpetuate that belief by measuring ourselves and others by that standard.

Judgment keeps us in line, and we internalize that as shame to stay compliant. We fear that we are not *good enough* to be in our power and allow our ego to mold an outward image so we don't have to confront it. The cycle of powerlessness multiplies infinitely until it is all that we see, all that we believe, and all that we teach the next generation—simply because we don't know better.

We've been shaped by 3D to such a degree that to know ourselves outside of it is almost impossible. So we have to burn it all out, as much as we don't want to. We have to look at every belief that tells us life has to look a certain way for it to be successful to know that it isn't the case. We have to take the tormented choices we made and replace them with peaceful ones. Although, for most people who have allowed judgment and shame to keep themselves and others in line, that looks crazy as hell.

To be fair, thinking we are *good enough* in this world is crazy. Being happy is an act of rebellion in a world where we are trapped in our fears and suffering. Being at peace is the ultimate Fuck You in a world that is ruled by creating and perpetuating our Shit. And being compassionate towards others and ourselves is the uprising in a world that tells us we are different, and those differences are something to fear.

But when we don't challenge the belief that this is how life is meant to be, when we follow the rules to stay safe, and when we deem our desires fantasy and impossible, we ensure they cannot be real in our world. We can never serve anything or anyone with our gifts and talents, least of all ourselves, when we run away from our Shit, doubts, and need for control—whilst negating our instincts and creating explanations before it is clear.

We may start our lives happy, but every moment we engage with 3D Separation, we absorb a new reason why we shouldn't be. But just as we perpetuate 3D Separation, we can also end it. And we start by finding the courage to admit that our lives in 3D are not working for us. However, we often stop ourselves from taking those small steps. We get lost in the details, and our minds mute our hearts out of the fear of uncertainty. This leaves us not only impotent to get to the bigger picture we want to experience but also narrows down what it could be like because we aren't discovering who we are and what suits us.

Following our joy doesn't have to fit in with what's been done before. The point isn't to perpetuate the world we know, it's to create one that works for us. That is how we change the collective. That is how we change our world. And that is how we ensure we don't repeat the Shitty patterns we've accepted for so long whilst patting ourselves on the back for the micro changes that seem to make a big difference but don't really change much at all.

We have to free ourselves of all the ways we live in the prison of 3D and accept it. It isn't freedom when there is a structure telling us what freedom looks like, even if it is disguised as "for our best interest as we don't know any better." If we still believe that someone else knows better, we won't give ourselves the chance to find out who we can really be. Everything else is just details.

I thought I was being a revolutionary in every aspect of my career, but I wasn't showing how anything was possible. Rather, I was showing how some other things could be possible if we gamed the system. Even worse, my first point (Love) was getting lost. I was perpetuating the lie that I was only good for helping others in a way that had already been done before.

To find my power, I needed to first see that I had any power at all. I didn't have to be an overworked cog in a dysfunctional machine, nor did I have to channel my dissatisfaction by focusing on a symptom rather than the cause. I had to allow for a different possibility than assuming that the most I could do was shift an existing system. Otherwise, I would always remain beholden to someone else's rules whilst wondering why I wasn't able to meaningfully facilitate anyone's freedom, including my own.

Do Wot You Do
Liz

Free will is true spiritual autonomy. We can exercise our choices any way we wish and make our lives as we want them to be. Free will is the choice that keeps us in 3D. It allows us to believe that we are separate from the Divine and to operate in a world where our reality supports that belief wherever we look.

In Separation, free will allows us to traverse the spectrum of highs and lows that 3D offers so we can partake in it all. It also gives us the illusion that we exist within a much larger framework because it doesn't seem as if there is much to stop us. But that is one of the many lies propagated by Separation. Even though we believe we are free to live as we want, the reality is that freedom is limited to what is available to us or what we perceive to be available.

That's the catch: the foundation of 3D (religion, government, and economic systems that form the tentpoles) makes sure that our freedoms are constantly curbed, because if not, our freedom would be a threat to their very survival. Whatever system we live under makes its subjects believe that everything they have and however they live is either enough or a sign of how deserving they are.

Yet, since it is the nature of the soul to be free, free will helps the soul navigate a life in Separation that it would otherwise find unbearable. It could be free enough, but only inasmuch that it could actualize the most adequate life possible without becoming fully self-actualized. In other words, it's as good as it's gonna get, which is really just settling.

While it may be human nature to settle, it's not the soul's nature to settle. Settling doesn't make us happy, it just makes us less unhappy and mitigates the fear that it could be and will likely be worse (see why #gratitude doesn't really work in *A Karmic Attraction*). To create a different experience, we need to take responsibility for how these choices nearly kill us and make us so fucking unhappy, listless, anxious, depressed, angry, scared, small, or powerless.

Karma forces us to face the Separation inside of ourselves, and there's no escaping it because we cannot escape ourselves. That's why karma's such an inescapable bitch. And that's why the only way out of our karmic loop is to make karma *our* bitch. Otherwise, our karma will wreak havoc to wake us up. That fear that *I Am not Good Enough* runs through our karmic story until we own our karmic issue and look at how it dictates the choices that keep us in Separation.

Neither of these is easy, but they are simple in that the moment we begin the process, things shift and opportunities present themselves for healing. Perhaps an old relationship that ended bitterly resurfaces in the form of the same person or another person. Maybe an opportunity to create abundance presents itself but requires a risk we've never considered, which challenges our carefully constructed routines. Or maybe the death of someone close forces us to reexamine everything we hold dear and compels us to view life differently.

However we begin, or whatever catalyst brings us to the starting point of this karmic misadventure, matters less than what we do while we're on it—namely, how readily we take advantage of all the opportunities for growth that come our way and how open we are to the multitude of lessons that present themselves.

Courage is truly living from the heart. We have played with notions of courage, from bravery to resilience, and from fortitude to determination. We've managed to "push through" and "weather storms." However, living from the heart takes everything to another level because it requires that we live from that space where Love informs our lives in their entirety.

The power that comes with living from the heart is our divine power. It's the gift we give ourselves the moment we transcend our karma and realize there's life after the pain and there's more to our existence than merely surviving. It's merely a stand-in for the Divine since our full divinity cannot exist in Separation. Only in 5D are we able to hold ourselves up in our own right (which requires us to be independent), take pride in who we are (own the lives we choose to lead), and have the self-respect to acknowledge that we are enough as we are (not to need any more than what we require to live our purpose).

When we operate from our divinity and exercise our divine power, it doesn't mean we retire from the temporal world and go find a mountaintop and Om ourselves until we die. If that were the case, Rhea most certainly wouldn't have signed on for this work. Rather, we take that personal power, compassion, and whole, healed self and live out our purpose.

While our distinct purpose is an expression of who we are as individuals, we all embody the same intention, which is to serve the collective. When we embody our divine selves and live from a place of harmony, we are serving others and, by extension, the world by helping it heal. All it requires is that we cease to hold ourselves in judgment and subsequent shame. In doing that, we eliminate all the judgment and shame that we fling out into the world. And the less judgment we hold, the more compassion we can cultivate.

Freedom

Since 2012, many of us have been consciously trying to reconnect to the Divine, little by little, casting off the layers of 3D that have kept us bound to the old world. Coming into this lifetime, right here, right now, means we have all chosen conscious awareness; it hurts so much to be in

Separation, and no soul wishes to remain unconscious. As a matter of fact, it's anathema to the soul's nature, which is to always be connected to the Divine.

The problem with free will, other than allowing us to delude ourselves, is that it gives us the power to *remain* separate from the Divine, which isn't really part of the deal. Free will is merely one of the few divine gifts (like the Law of Attraction) souls can use in 3D (a bit like a survival kit for Separation). It enables the soul to maintain as much autonomy as possible while in human body, to act within the rules of Separation *as well as* to adhere to its divine nature, which is having as much freedom to create and destroy. This latter notion is key to the fundamental nature of free will, which allows any soul to act as it sees fit while in body.

Our egos do the best job they can by helping us survive Separation. Their greatest skill is that they recognize how to best keep us in line with whatever rules govern our world and help us make the best of our lives while making it seem like it's all we want. But it's not what we really want, it's merely the best we can get, and the ego understands that. As long as there is some version of *good enough* that we can settle for, then we never have to experience the big fallout of discovering that we're *not at all good enough* could really mean.

Free will is the ego's greatest weapon in keeping our core fear at bay and, by extension, alive because it limits our freedom to mitigate our fears (if we don't completely deal with a fear, it doesn't go away). As a result, we remain stuck in Separation, so the ego remains relevant. But this is when humanity self-destructs.

Our freedom to act becomes lost to the ego, which seeks to control our fears, and if we can't be the determinant of our own lives, we lose our will to live. Our human experience ceases to be a total free-for-all and becomes siphoned through the 3D lens of polarity. Everything that we apply to our lives, actions, and choices is no longer as free as we thought. They carry the weight and burden of purpose, meaning, and virtue that revolve around the tentpoles of 3D. As a result, free will is no longer free; it becomes a distorted mechanism for the ego.

The ego maintains a false sense of independence, and it reinforces the lie that we know better. Worst of all, it uses our free will against us. Rather than throwing caution to the wind and allowing that will to take us on a wild ride through 3D, it tries to harness divine energy and narrowly directs it to fit within the confines of Separation. So free will, which began as a way for us to exercise what divinity we could in 3D and explore all that was possible in this Wild West of the universe, became co-opted by our egos to keep us small and safe. Thus, we can only be safe, successful, and happy in the only way our egos would have us believe we could be in 3D.

To be fair, humanity is so used to the shackles of 3D that it doesn't know true freedom, which is why it holds onto the ego for dear life. But the desire to control, predict, anticipate, and maintain certainty runs against our soul's nature to be free. We didn't come here to be small and safe. We came here to realize our God-selves in the face of Separation, and free will was meant to remind us that we carry within each of us the ability to be our own God and create the lives we wish.

If we can see our fears are only as real as we allow them to be, we can see that so much of our lives is a construct to support this illusion. When we can see through the construct, we can grasp that freedom we had before the ego turned on us and made us believe that we couldn't live outside the lines of polarity. This is when we can begin to explore the possibilities that reside on the other side of Separation, where Oneness lies.

There is no room for free will in the unknown. Not because free will abhors uncertainty like the ego but because free will is born from the ability to create Separation. That same ability defines, labels, categorizes, or makes space. In other words, it holds Otherness, and we maintain the energy of Otherness through the act of differentiation.

Oneness, however, doesn't differentiate. There are no discernible differences when we are at One because when we recognize the Divine in ourselves and others, everything else becomes surface distinction. We had to see what our ability to operate in human form with limited divine connection has done to our world and the glorious mess that results.

This is why we're so fixated on relationships and love, whether they are fantasy or real. We don't forget that connection by happenstance. We have been working towards Oneness by burning out our capacity to separate. It is a mess because our egos don't want to let go of their significance. They have so much influence over our choices because we continue to hold on to fear and project that fear outward, victimizing ourselves in the process. Our egos are the reason we are our own greatest enemy and self-sabotage left, right, and center. Our egos lead us to believe that we are useless without them and reinforce our fear that if we can't control our thoughts and actions, then we are hapless victims of our own fate.

When we are our most divine selves, neither words, feelings, nor thoughts can describe us. It can exist without ego, rules, labels, definitions, or judgment. When we reach this power, our need for free will diminishes because free will is actually a weak substitute for our divinity. Freedom isn't about compromise; it's about being able to live our lives without compromise. We don't have to compromise when we become clear about who we are, why we're here, and what we choose to do with our lives.

Eternal Flame
Rhea

My karma showed me where I wasn't listening to myself, where I lacked the confidence to apply my own rules (rather than someone else's), and it forced me to step up and own who I was rather than squash myself into a box. But it also did more than that. It showed me how to navigate the way out and beyond.

My choice was simple: to live as me rather than die hiding. I decided to give myself a chance to achieve everything I desired because I knew that there was more joy to find. I chose to believe the part of me that knew better, that filled my heart with light, and that made me excited to live, even if it was just for a moment. The more I leant into one moment, the more they multiplied until I had filled my world with the light that I had been hellbent on denying for so long.

To understand the implications of this choice and fully accept that I was no longer who I had been—and, as a result, that I had to live accordingly to find peace— changed everything. I finally understood that being able to choose is freedom, and being fearless when making that choice is power. That was when my life opened up to meaningful relationships and my connection to my divinity—so the rest could flow from there.

In *A Karmic Attraction*, we explained that purpose is not our reason for living but *what* underpins that reason. Our reason for living is us. We are on this earth to have the greatest experience that we can conceive and more. But whilst our purpose can offer a great deal of joy and motivation, it's not the source of our joy but merely an expression of it. Purpose is how we express our joy because when we fully embody it, we are sourced by Love.

In *A Karmic Affair*, we shared that Love, the act of shining our light for others to see, drives us forward to our purpose. But whilst we can skirt around our purpose, tap into facets of it, or even express it in a small way, we can't embrace it fully until we have embraced our power. Until we can see that our purpose doesn't necessarily live within the confines of what has been done before, we will continue to limit it for fear that we will get it wrong whilst expecting certain results.

We may think that writing a book will bring us the meaning we seek or helping others will offer a reason for our existence, but that will leave us wanting if it's not sourced from a place of power. But when we engage meaningfully with our purpose, which can look like those exact pursuits, we can uncover who we are and what we are capable of.

We're not here to be the people we were or shinier versions of them, we're here to be more. We're here to be everything we want to be, even if we can't fully articulate or identify what exactly that means, because we still have some pieces to gather or experiences to help shape us. We are here to experience that full self in every conceivable way we desire—simply because we aren't holding ourselves back anymore.

This isn't some effort to excuse our pasts or say we know better and erase our history. It's acknowledging that we get to a point along that growth and evolution spectrum (that Liz refers to), that who we were and what we went through is so far away from who we are that they almost seem like multiple past lives. We know we had them and that we experience things as a result of them, but they just aren't that important anymore. If anything, they are a barrier to our freedom, not a reason why we are free.

This does not erase or negate our pasts. On the contrary, it shows us how far we can go and that we really can experience everything that we dream of. The difference is simply how we do it and what we allow ourselves to achieve. But the more we hold ourselves to an outdated standard of behavior or measure ourselves against some bar we created when we didn't believe in ourselves, the more we deny ourselves the opportunity to see our potential.

That's why we need to blitz the Separation within so that we can eradicate the Separation without. We've been conditioned to believe that our purpose is tangible and is in a singular role, passion, or exploit. It's outside of us and defined by what we produce and who we affect. It's become our reason for living. However, in allowing it to remain small, we have remained small with it.

It isn't one type of relationship, institution, or career that needs fixing, it's everything that is based on lack, fear, and the perpetuation of an imbalance of power (where one has one over the other). Life in Separation doesn't just strip us of our fundamental right to self-determination, it strips us of our agency and power. That doesn't just leave us shouting into a void, it leaves us with no hope of escaping. Until we can see that it's all a lie, we will keep propping it up simply by behaving like we need it.

Now, this is not a manifesto on living off the grid, growing our own food, communing with our own God, and getting off social media. Those things could be great, if that is what we are so inclined to do, but we are relational beings, and coexisting is supposed to be a joy, not a burden. We are meant to see our light reflected in each other and bring our hearts together to create something new that we haven't experienced before. We know that. Otherwise, we wouldn't be shouting about the injustices we see or trying to protect those that are hurt.

We can be even better than the *better enough* that we have become. We can fill our worlds with joy because we are in joy, and we can take responsibility for our lives without assuming responsibility for anyone else's. Our purpose depends on this. We don't need to come to terms with the people we used to be, we need to have compassion for our own decisions to abandon or reject ourselves. Other people have never defined us, even when they patted us on the back or tried to cut us off at the knees.

Our purpose is an expression of how we make our joy present because it's what we create as a result of our light, not the other way around. We don't need to listen to someone else to know whether something is right for us, we don't need someone else to tell us where our boundaries lie, and we definitely don't need anyone to explain to us how to share our hearts. They are ours. No matter how we choose to know, own, and express ourselves, it is always more than enough. When we realize this, then the judgment and shame that keeps 3D in place cannot keep us trapped in it anymore.

Time After Time

What we are looking for always starts with us because the bigger the idea we can hold, the greater the experience we can have. That sounds scary because, in some ways, it means that everything that is perpetuating our disempowerment must be redefined. But if we allow it to unfold in line with our evolution, it will feel natural—until we get to a place where we understand that we don't need the expectations and limiting safeguards that 3D provides.

This doesn't happen overnight. To truly come into our power takes time—time I didn't believe I had because I was too busy pushing against some arbitrary deadlines on what I needed to achieve and when. And whilst in some ways I was a massive overachiever (who helps to change a domestic violence law at 31?), in others, I was floundering (who can't support themselves at 31?). But the more I judged myself for failing to reach socially acceptable milestones whilst celebrating others like I was some sort of genius, the more the clock dictated my success.

I couldn't see that everything was unfolding in a way that was perfect for me, so I made time my enemy. Except time wasn't my enemy, and it wasn't ruling me at all. I did everything that I needed to do, and I still had time to do what I wanted as well. In fact, the only time I struggled was when I stopped to look at the clock and wondered what it meant for me.

I was scared of a clock that I wasn't engaging with. Time was just a specter that had cast a shadow over my choices and caused me to doubt my path. It wasn't out to get me, as much as I told myself otherwise. I had just internalized others' perceptions of what I should be doing and when I should be doing it.

If I had stayed working at the law firm, I would have followed the prescribed steps to a prescribed end game. I would have known exactly what was required of me to progress to the next stage of my career and what that would look like when I got there. I could look to my superiors to know who to emulate and compare my salary with my peers to know if I was getting ripped off. Sure, that would have been safe. But it wouldn't have been remotely interesting, and I wouldn't have achieved as much as I did coloring outside the lines.

That's the thing about the 3D timeline. It's safe. It's predictable. And for some people, that's a gift that they don't take for granted. But fuck if it's not limiting. We are always one second away from losing it all because we've sent the wrong email or said the wrong thing that we couldn't preempt. Time ceases to be a gateway to potential and instead threatens inevitable loss. So, we hold on to every moment like it's our last whilst trying to control the next one so that another one may come—only to do the whole thing again.

That's the treadmill that we can't get off—trying to avoid fucking up but panicking that we will in the next moment, ad infinitum. It's draining, it's tiring, and it makes us feel like we can never be *good enough* because we can only hope to survive another day. We are constantly waiting for the other shoe to drop and telling ourselves that it's only good until it gets bad. Not because it will but because it has to. At some point, our lucky streak will end, and instead of picking up the pieces, we'll be stuck wondering what the moment that killed it was.

In accepting that I didn't want my life to look like the future I'd been working towards, I'd freed myself from the constraints of the 3D timeline, even if I hadn't clocked it at the time. Sure, it appeared that I had no idea what I was doing, but not playing in the rat race meant I never had to play by their rules. I only had to play by mine. I didn't have to worry that someone else could pull the rug from under me because, frankly, there was no rug.

When I said yes to working in domestic violence, I was presented with more chances to say yes. That allowed me to tap into my desire for justice and make a difference in a way that made sense to me. When I said yes to the podcast with Liz, I was able to say yes to the books that followed and ultimately learn a different way to approach my life. Every time I said yes, more chances to say yes were presented. I didn't get bored waiting for the proverbial payoff. Instead, the payoff came at every stage. Every moment I did something new or took a risk, I found a chance for better than before. In doing so, time became an agent of my growth rather than an agent of my demise.

When I looked back, I could see that not only had everything unfolded in a way that I couldn't have premeditated, but I ended up precisely where it served me best, even if it wasn't necessarily where I expected. I didn't find the right opportunity at a job interview or show up at the right networking event. I found it by doing what I enjoyed and letting things unfold from there. Whether it was a chance meeting through a friend of a friend, a trip to the nail salon, or even a random DM, the next step in my career always found me, not the other way around. I didn't need to make my life happen by being in the right place at the right time. I just had to acknowledge that I wanted more and say yes when it arrived.

That's the beauty of working with time rather than against it. It becomes a mechanism for opportunity rather than a ball on a long and heavy chain that we have to drag around. In releasing myself from arbitrary deadlines that may have been safe but were extremely limiting, I allowed myself the chance to see what I was really capable of. By expanding my consciousness so that I was no longer bound by a ticking clock, I used the freedom that had been with me all along to create what I desired. That may have started with finding my light and shining it, but it continued as I followed that light wherever it led. That was how I created my world and ensured that it would be better than the one that came before it.

One Way Or Another
Liz

While Separation assumes that free will is too dangerous a power for the average person to have because it makes them destructive and evil, Oneness understands that we are incapable of destroying or harming others because it would be the same as destroying ourselves. This values-based system is difficult to comprehend now because we apply much of our 3D thinking that pits good against evil, virtue against vice, and right against wrong. But the absence of polarity accepts that everything just is, and the framework for our interaction is neither competition nor struggle but compassion and harmony.

To establish the 5D framework, Oneness consciousness demands we bear witness to the past to put it to rest. This does not mean shaming or rewriting it because that only serves to bring the past into the present, which keeps it alive. Instead, we hold it and laugh, cry, or scream at the injustice of all that pain. Only then can we release it and ourselves from the bounds of 3D. When we heal our past and accept it as it was, it no longer keeps those experiences in Separation. That is how we heal Separation without destroying our humanity in the process.

It will take time to have the critical mass necessary for harmony to be the overriding logos for much of our world. The divisions between races, classes, religions, cultures, ideologies, and politics will grow further apart before future generations bridge them. This is because 3D consciousness still permeates much of our structures, and it will take time to dismantle them. Breaking them down all at once would create too much instability, and that would be unproductive and messy. That would lead us to spend more of our time and energy cleaning up the mess of the past as opposed to laying the foundation for our future.

While there may not be enough critical mass for our world to be covered in harmony, there is enough to enable the collective consciousness necessary to bring it to fruition. And for now, that is enough. For anyone who wishes to do more, here are the steps for positioning ourselves to hold Oneness consciousness:

1. Accept that reality is an ever-shifting concept.

What is true for one person isn't necessarily true for another. This can create quite a dissonance for some who are very wedded to polarity. This dissonance often triggers an emotional response because many of us cannot tolerate the idea of multiple realities because they run counter to the 3D experience that has informed much of who we are. Yet the sooner we accept that there are so many realities, and our own is merely one of the possibilities, the sooner we come into harmony with our surrounding world.

2. Understand that our lives are not as unique as we are inclined to believe.

The pain and fear that underscores how we experience our lives tell us that no one could possibly understand what it's like to be us, either because of our gender, sexual orientation, ethnicity, race, past trauma, or family bonds (the list is long because humankind has such a lengthy, prominent history of victimhood). But the truth is that behind all the various masks of victimization lies a singular experience that we all share: Separation. We have all been winners and losers in this game, and no one is exempt from it, no matter how things appear on the surface. Some are merely better at hiding it, but so long as we live a life in Separation, we hold the principles of Otherness, which impact and hurt us all.

3. To hope for better.

Hope reflects our deepest desires. These desires are our compass. They point the way to our purpose and the underlying meaning of all our lives. That meaning is why we are here—to realize our greatest self, which is our innermost divine being. And that divine being speaks many languages and comes in all colors, shapes, and sizes, along with a variety of gifts and talents. The contentment and peace that come with living according to our deepest desires are what we put out in the world, and they have a multiplier effect. We just need to remember that change of any kind always begins with being the person we most want to be, regardless of what others do or think. That takes courage, something we are only now coming to understand. Courage doesn't come out of the blue. Nor does it arrive at the precise moment we need it. It's the result of slowly healing the holes in our hearts that appear when we first experience Separation.

That trauma and heartbreak happen when we realize we are no longer at One with the Divine. When our hearts are broken, we lack the wherewithal and the courage to act on our own behalf. So instead of following our heart's desire, we follow what we think our heart is missing, such as the One.

We might wonder that if we're so divine, then there's got to be an easier way to be free from Separation. While there is, karma is the most efficient way to move our consciousness from one state to another without fully annihilating ourselves. We can no longer support or live in Separation because it is destroying our humanity. As indifferent or critical as some may regard the human race or our very humanity, the truth is that our humanity is what makes us unique.

Yes, yes, our souls are unique expressions of the Divine, and that's really cool considering the make-up of a soul and where it's been over lifetimes and in multi-dimensional spaces, but let's not forget how sweet and awesome human life is—how our emotional spectrum really bonds us, from the joys and the love to the sadness and closeness we gain through our humanity. There's something so equally beautiful and hopeful about the precious messiness of our individual and collective human stories over eons that to wipe it all away would be a greater loss than many realize.

Don't You (Forget About Me)

Up until now, we've all been a shadow of a person (not to be confused with *shadow self*, that's *A Karmic Attraction* stuff). We've barely scratched the surface of who this person is meant to be because it's too soon. While it would've been nice and certainly spared us a lot of time, not to mention be incredibly efficient in maintaining our profound divine connection from birth, it wouldn't have been possible to sustain it over a long period. Separation would inevitably rear its ugly head, and we would eventually succumb to judgment.

It's not for lack of trying. Rather, it's because our karma and our human nature—which carries the core fear, *I Am not Good Enough*—would always ensure that we would live with a specter, a monkey on our backs, to remind us that we're less than perfect. If we have to carry our perceived sense of perfection through our divinity while living with the constant reminder of our imperfections, the dissonance will cause us to split even more than we already have.

Consciousness is when three of our bodies fully align. Our physical, mental, and emotional bodies all need to be functioning harmoniously and effortlessly for us to become conscious beings. The only way for these three bodies to align with one another is by eliminating the fear that separates them.

As creative beings, we are incredibly adept at assuring ourselves we're adapting while hardly changing a thing. That is why we have been in such a crisis. We have had to bear witness to this suffering throughout our lifetime to heal it. We have had to face all the ways we let ourselves down to ensure that we could frame this karmic period of our lives, tie it up with a bow, and burn it. It hasn't been easy because it's uncomfortable, which is why many would rather forget and why many have forgotten.

We forget so that we can remember, because that remembering is the point. As we remember, or *re-member*, ourselves and put ourselves back together, the knowing comes back to us. That sense of power, divinity, and connection returns, and we're reminded of why we're here. That's the express purpose of karma: to get us to remember and achieve a higher level of consciousness.

We are still in the process of remembering who we are, and until we remember fully and piece ourselves back together, we cannot live the lives we are meant to live. We get there by allowing all the possibilities written into our fate to surface.

Fate is the roadmap by which we live our lives (in *A Karmic Attraction*, I called it a tapestry; the visual is the same, I'm just trying to keep it interesting for everyone.). There is absolutely nothing random about our lives, despite what we may be inclined to believe. Yet, we are the ones who write this map. Moreover, we are the ones who ensure we live according to our fate. That's what our Guides are here for, and our karma helps preserve it, ensuring we stay on our fate.

Fate directs us through our most expanded life path possible and can only be realized when we are fully present in our lives. There are a multitude of roads, left and right turns, one-way streets, alleyways and footpaths—as many as our eyes can perceive. Like the tapestry, there is a series of paths, one more intricate than the other, woven and layered, with different scenes and images, all somewhat connected but seemingly disparate patterns.

Fate, in its vast layout, is grand and beautiful because it is perfectly designed for us by us. When we are in our karma, we exist within a very narrow portion of this map, which is what we know as our destiny. We stay in our lanes or a specific part of the picture as we play through our karmic story. Everything we experience, including all our relationships, reflects that larger roadmap intended to bring us to freedom.

When we divest ourselves of our karma, the map or tapestry can reveal itself, and we see the vast possibilities before us—hence why we may be inclined to make big life changes at certain junctures in our lives. We may find that we've outgrown something or someone, and we're ready for a new challenge or opportunity that we may not have yet perceived before. We'll know when we reach this because things will begin to feel stagnant in at least three of the four possible pathways we have running through our fate, whether they be with work, relationships, purpose, or mission. So when we experience this, we call forth new challenges to move us forward through the various points along our fate.

We can only reach this point when we've fully emptied ourselves of everything about our old lives that represented our karma. There is absolutely nothing about our karmic story that is meant to remain. Even our relationships cannot be what they were. If they stay, they, too, must evolve and change. Only what is meant for our fate will endure, and that ensures that how we live our lives always stays in line with what we've written for ourselves.

The Next Episode
Rhea

My career was one of the few places where I wasn't drowning in my Shit. However, when I started the work with Liz, I acted like it was all about allowing others access to the Guides when really it was an attempt to deal with my personal Shit. I believed that the more I learnt about how the universe worked, the more I could use it to my advantage.

What I learnt is that it's all Shit: the Shit that happens, the Shit we perpetuate, and the Shit we create when we've run out of Shit to work through. I produced podcasts, wrote books, made snazzy meditation music, and waved my pendulum about to check that I was on the right track. But, in doing so, every one of my own insecurities came out, I became a workaholic out of fear rather than joy, and the time it took to edit a podcast increased tenfold because I was so busy making it about my own life.

I also started allowing the work to control me. I created arbitrary deadlines where I told myself that if I edited just one more episode, finished one more chapter, or completed one more lesson, then the old me (the one who was very dramatic about how Shit her life was) would die, and a new, shiny, magnetic version would stand in her place.

I constantly asked questions during recording sessions because I wanted to know what I was doing wrong, and then I immediately dismissed the answers because my doubts made more sense. I would edit the podcasts and hope to fix the final issue that was holding me back, only to find another one in the next episode. I would write a chapter and tell myself that this would be the chapter that changed everything, only to find it didn't change very much at all.

Sure, I got answers, but that didn't mean as much as one would think because they weren't the answers I sought. My knowing may have told me that my perspective was the issue, but as I didn't shift my lens away from Separation, I made it my fault rather than taking responsibility. In doing so, the work became another way to self-flagellate whilst tricking myself into believing I would be forever trapped in my own Shit.

As we explained in *A Karmic Affair,* every relationship, even the one with our work, is showing us our karma, ego, and fear as much as it is showing us our light. But whilst we've explained extensively that just as light attracts light, fear attracts fear, what we haven't explained is how.

Sure, Liz can give some extremely interesting answers about energy and the Law of Attraction, but there is another way of looking at it. I wasn't ruled by the work, I wasn't ruled by Guidance, and I definitely wasn't ruled by Liz. I created the work, and in doing so, I decided how that impacted me. I wanted to learn and figure out what was stopping me from living the life I knew to be possible, so I allowed myself to see all the ways in which that was being manifested. I already knew all those "deep-seated" fears that I was disguising as a revelation because I had been carrying them around with me. I was just using the work to see my issues in a different context.

I'm not talking about reflecting some old pain we haven't dealt with. I'm saying that every relationship we have shows us where we are holding ourselves back from our power. On some level, I knew I was powerful whilst denying that I had any power at all. I made myself feel powerless to break out of my prison whilst finding a sliver of light at the end of the tunnel. Except I wasn't finding freedom, I was sticking my head out of the window of a padded cell.

That's the insidious thing about karma, Separation, and all the bullshit we put ourselves through—we buy into the lie that to learn is to suffer and that suffering never ends. We just get better at enduring everything or slapping a gratitude sticker over it, hoping the lesson doesn't find us again. And yes, as I said in the introduction of *A Karmic Attraction*, Shit happens to everyone. But it doesn't have to happen forever. Once we see how powerful we are and the many possibilities ahead of us, we don't have to take more Shit.

I may have believed that the work was foreshadowing the next painful episode, but it wasn't. It was simply shining a light on a part of me that I was still keeping in the dark. That is why it felt so accurate and why I felt I was a plaything of something much larger than me. The work was light, but to match it, I had to see where I was giving my power away. Until I could understand that there was nothing wrong with me and take responsibility for my life, I would forever find new and exciting ways to prove that I couldn't change my life in any meaningful way. Every season of the podcast and every book we would write wouldn't bring me closer to seeing the truth until I was ready to see it for myself.

Blaze Of Glory

Everything we experience is used to back up the story that we tell ourselves, regardless of what that story is. I didn't believe that I could listen to myself and create my world, I thought that someone had to deliver it to me or that I had to work *really* hard to earn it. And because karma can truly be a bitch, especially when the work is based on making it your bitch—I finally had enough of the Shit, so I quit.

I may have been excellent at making excuses for others whilst silencing my own needs, but I couldn't do it anymore. I was resentful, scared to death that I was placing my energy into something that didn't seem reliable, and exhausted from waiting for the other shoe to drop on my face and knock me out. I didn't know how to abandon all the beliefs I had spent the past years cultivating, but I also didn't know how to justify it, either. If I couldn't tick the achievements off my list, then I thought I had nothing. That meant, for me, the work wasn't enough.

We aren't meant to lament our pain until we curse ourselves into the ground with it. That's what many of us do, though. We tell ourselves that our problems aren't going anywhere and there is no point in trying, or we push them off to another day and take the path of least resistance because it is what we've always known. I'd assumed that in wanting one thing, I had to sacrifice everything else until I had it. But that's the opposite of what true spirituality is. It exists to remind us we always have a choice and that we need to maintain our freedom so that we can exercise that choice whenever it's right for us.

Often, we don't know how to do something differently because we don't believe we can be different. We look at what we want our lives to look like and tell ourselves we aren't capable of getting there, or we don't want to take responsibility because we would have to deal with what comes next—it feels so unfamiliar that we don't think we can handle it. But if the only person standing in the way of my freedom was me, and it was always me, then it was up to me to figure out why I kept missing my point.

The work wasn't enough because I asked it to provide something it could never do. I'd created the prison in which I was living whilst expecting someone or something else to break me out of it. But even when I was given all the tools to free myself, I was still searching for the next lesson, the next fall, and bracing myself for impact. Turns out that even the most amazing things that we engage with can become toxic.

When I told Liz that I was done, there was no drama or fanfare or questions on her end. There was no prison at all. She immediately said I didn't have to continue the work and reminded me that I always had a choice. That's when I realized I was free to make my own choices, and I always had been. In recognizing that, I finally gave myself the chance to choose consciously.

Did I enjoy recording the podcast and laughing with my friend? Absolutely. Did I enjoy the rush of writing a book? Definitely. Did I enjoy learning and expanding and having experiences I'd never had before? Always. Did I enjoy going out and dancing all night with a cute boy? Every time. But did I enjoy betraying myself repeatedly because I didn't feel like I was *good enough*? Never.

My expectations created a world where I couldn't even recognize that because I was too busy measuring it against what I thought my life should look like. So, every time I worried about a future that may not come, judged a present that looked alternative, or lamented a past that should have been different, I dropped out of joy. Turns out my expectations for what my life *should* look like, what *should* bring me joy, and how I *should* be living were hurting me, and I didn't even realize it—simply because I was still waiting for this #dreamlife before I even knew what my dreams were. It wasn't the payoff that would come later, it was the experience itself.

I must have said the words "blaze of glory" about a hundred times in Liz's kitchen when I realized that I couldn't walk away from our work because that would mean I would also be walking away from myself. I didn't want to spend the rest of my life wondering, and I'd had enough of thinking I wasn't *good enough* to make my own fucking choices. If I walked away before knowing whether my feelings were bullshit or real, I wouldn't be able to live with myself. I needed to give myself a chance to see what would happen if I jumped in with both feet. Otherwise, I would never know if my issues had been driven by fear.

I showed up for myself because when I realized I was free to choose the work for myself, I did. I wasn't choosing Karma's My Bitch because I was at my lowest emotional state and clinging onto something to stop me from getting lower; I was actually jumping into the unknown and believing I could handle whatever came next. Of the two options available to me, walking away was far easier. By taking a risk, I wasn't letting my doubts and insecurities govern my life.

When I recorded the podcast for answers, I ended up continuously searching for them. When I wrote books expecting they would change my life, I found my life unchanged. But when I accepted I would do both of those things regardless of what they would deliver to me, I discovered more than my limited mind could have foreseen. In connecting to what brought me joy regardless of the result, I allowed myself to expand that joy to bring it into everything that I engaged with.

Knowing Me, Knowing You
Liz

We have been invited to examine all the ways our labels and teachings within Separation keep us battling ourselves and one another. It's not that we're meant to become different from who we are now, we're merely meant to become more of that awesome self that we already know ourselves to be but have stifled, muted, gagged, or altered to fit within the bounds of 3D consciousness.

It seems like a lot to grasp, especially if we've only been recently working on our karmic Shit. This is because if we were really to awaken to Separation at once, it would quite literally destroy us because a soul cannot exist outside of wholeness. To enable a soul to move from Separation to Oneness, we use one of seven karmic themes that underscore our karmic stories. Separation and all of its rules keep us complacent by robbing us of our power. Separation tells us life sucks, and then we die. Karma says, "fuck that." It also says, "anything is better than this."

Not only do we have karma, which fast-tracks anyone looking to transform their current reality and design one for themselves, but we also have the benefit of the whole world falling apart at the same time, so we no longer have the tentpoles to provide refuge from the Shitstorm.

While Separation literally separates us from ourselves and others, the complete unraveling of Separation around us has given us no ledge to grasp onto. It feels like one big freefall without a parachute. That's been the point all along. Nothing was ever going to save us.

But we should have seen it, and we should've known. We were warned. Our recent histories of injustices, strife, destruction, and intolerance pointed to it. There would be a reckoning. There would come a time when all the values and promises of 3D would turn on humankind, and we would be thrust into this netherworld of hopelessness and despair, with uncertainty clouding our many days, strung together by nothing more than the grief over the fact that all we'd ever known would never return.

This is not karma's fault. One thing that humankind is quite gifted at is denial. Spoon-feed anyone enough positive mindset platitudes, and many will want to follow you. We forgot that we were powerful enough to create this mess all on our own—and powerful enough to ensure there was no escaping it until we faced our Shit.

In recognizing the karmic game for what it is, we are accepting there are no more rules (this is exciting for some who hate rules and hugely challenging for people who can't live without them). It might be difficult for some to get their heads around this, which is understandable. Separation is not only rules-based, it's also outcome-based. In walking a particular path, we expect to reach a certain outcome. That predictability gives us the comfort in knowing that whatever we do, so long as we do it correctly, all will be well. However, it stops us from living fully.

Separation offers us the false assurance that if we follow a few rules, we'll be safe and happy, but we never really are since the rules to keep us safe and happy are conditional. Separation teaches us that if we do X, then Y will result, but if Y doesn't result (often it doesn't), then we have to try harder, work more, or believe that it's all our fault (because you know, what goes around comes around) or that someone else dropped the ball (which makes us wrong for trusting them).

But how could we be surprised by a catastrophe when it's the very hallmark of 3D? As the Divine in body, if we are not exercising our power to create, we are exercising that power to destroy. When our power becomes stifled or distorted, as it has by 3D and our egos, then that destruction turns into self-destruction, which our impotence magnifies.

Since 2016, every bit of our karma has been up for careful examination. While our core issue is always *I Am not Good Enough* and presents in a variety of themes and stories, the ultimate lesson will always be the same. That lesson is: *I Am More than I Believe Myself to Be*. The crux of this is our divine identity.

While our divine identity acknowledges that we are just as much a part of the Divine as the Divine is part of us, it can be understood in three layers, which are listed from the innermost to the outermost layer.

1. The divine core.

This is the part of us that connects to all of creation (not just the Divine). It's true Oneness consciousness: nothing separates us from anyone or anything else. Our awareness of this divine core comes in the form of pure peace and can only be experienced by ourselves. It cannot be facilitated or shared with anyone else. This is the nucleus of our very existence and divine knowing that reminds us that there is a part of us that is wholly immutable and perfect.

2. The Divine in action.

The Divine creates to experience itself. One of the greatest attributes of 5D is creation, which can only be enabled when a soul has set about its highest purpose. To do this requires complete, full-bodied consciousness. Only then will the Divine be fully expressed in all that we are, say, and do.

3. The Divine in thought.

This is the greatest challenge of coming into our divine identities. It requires a kind of unequivocal self-belief in our relationship to the Divine *as well as* our capacity to own that relationship until it becomes our overriding logos—or rather, the alpha and omega of our very being. When we can achieve this, we enter full Oneness.

That is freedom. The freedom to be, think, and act according to our own system of values and exercise them as we see fit. But, like anything new, we don't quite feel we're ready for it. It's scary, it's not what we're used to, and it lacks the safety net we've all been deluded into thinking will catch us should we ever fall into 3D, when the reality is that Separation never comes with a safety net. (It was always just us navigating the potholes and managing the best we could.) But the Divine doesn't require a safety net. A safety net presumes there will be failure and prepares for the possibility of doom. A divine reality, on the other hand, knows and trusts that all will always be well *and* that the experience matters more than the outcome.

We experience and witness a fuck-ton of shifts before we land anywhere near 5D Oneness. Every single person on this planet at any given time has their own individual karmic process to go through. Since Oneness consciousness leaves no person behind, we loop through layers of our 3D consciousness as we process old 3D thinking, practices, and mores. This pushes us to the very limits of 3D, where it has to be burned out. None of this has been or will be easy. While we may not be responsible for every individual's choices or struggles, we are responsible for how we respond to them.

However, we always get what is coming, and we don't come into body in this lifetime to remain the pawns of Separation. We may not be experts at Oneness for a good portion of our lifetimes, but we need to develop enough consciousness so that it can be the prevailing ethos within our family units, communities, and cities.

We are primarily here to establish this foundation for future generations, who can only be born into a world with enough consciousness to support their divinity. Otherwise, there would be no point. There would be no need to push for the evolution of humanity because if it cannot evolve, it will self-destruct.

3D has been in place for far too long to see a new world rebuilt in a day. So 5D requires a period of transition while we emerge in our consciousness and heal our Shit, all the while we remain in body. While Oneness requires individual consciousness to contribute to collective consciousness, it does not mean thinking, being, or acting the same. It's about the individual contributing their unique gifts and talents to make this world what it can be.

Pandora's Box

Few of us really know who we are apart from our genders, inclinations, activities, education, titles, relationships, work, and economic class. We've gone so long layering our labels, one on top of the other, that removing them and getting to the core of who we really are feels like a game of Jenga, where if we take out one wrong piece, the entire structure will fall. So we've been careful, too careful, with our pieces—superficially dealing with our Shit but not really holding the entire piece in our hands in case everything comes crashing down.

This is why our collective 3D-to-5D transition has had a rocky, explosive start. There was no way of making it harmonious because we weren't in harmony with a damn thing, whether it be with one another, our environment, our relationships, our well-being, or within our financial and political institutions. We have been so devoid of peace in pretty much every area of our lives that waking us up to Oneness feels like a nuclear implosion throughout our bodies.

Since 2012, our consciousness around our feelings of fulfillment (or lack thereof) has steered us towards the end of 3D. Most of us were completely unaware of what was to come and what was due to arrive. There was such a sense of collective shock followed by grief that it was easy to wonder, "Is this what the end of days is supposed to feel like?" It certainly signified the end of something.

And yes, while the obvious answer is that it signified the end of 3D Separation, it also signified the end of who we thought ourselves to be. With the tentpoles of religion, government, and economic systems falling apart faster than our own lives, we literally cannot look to them to ensure our spiritual, physical, or financial well-being. So, while it feels like they're hanging us out to dry, the reality is that for the first time in all of our human incarnations, we are finally in a position to see just what we're made of.

Despite our best efforts, 3D Separation has been crumbling and will continue to crumble until we have our make-or-break moment when we are forced to confront what will make us fearless. To be fearless is not the same as having courage. Instead, it's the ability to live according to our divine identity, which is only possible with a whole, healed heart.

The more of our Separation identity we can cast off, the more we can see just how it feeds the illusion of our personal freedom. And the more of our divine identity we assume, the more we crave true freedom, which is to be, think, and act in accordance with our values. Yet, life in 3D is very seductive. We need to know we matter. We'll virtue signal, suck up, or deliberately gaslight to assert any influence we believe we have.

Humankind needs to be ready for the light, or it won't heal enough to make the most of it. That's what triggered the Shitstorm at the start of the 3D-to-5D transition. Humanity wasn't ready. It's a bit like preparing to go on holiday, having already purchased and planned the entire trip, but then realizing that the flight is due to leave in the next hour and that you've not packed a single item. All of a sudden, everything gets flung out of closets and drawers and haphazardly shoved into every available space. It's hard to be certain if the relevant items made it, but there's no time to think about it. It's time to go.

But it isn't that easy because Oneness consciousness requires that we be in full-body consciousness. Unlike past revolutions, which were about usurping a tyrant or establishing a new regime, this one isn't about firing the first shot or overthrowing our way of life. Rather, it is meant to reflect our personal evolution.

No one has to operate from this consciousness—yet. It would get those Oneness seeds planted sooner, but to say *I Am Enough* is truly enough. By holding space, we merely allow for the possibility of grasping the concept of Oneness consciousness. We grasp this by being open-minded *and* open-hearted enough to see ourselves in others and acknowledge that all that has ever separated us from one another is the artificial belief that we are not connected.

Show Me Love
Rhea

At the beginning of *A Karmic Affair*, I said that experiencing Love and sharing it are the main reasons I live. But my ego had created a version of my purpose, and I subscribed to it. It took what I knew about love and morphed it into a lifelong commitment, planning exactly how it would manifest and the necessary steps to get there.

That's partly why I so readily agreed to go on the podcast and took it all so damn seriously; I thought that through the podcast, I'd figure out how to find the right person to partner up with, whom I'd parade around like a badge of honor, advising others how to do the same. If I had some issues along the way, I would solve them in real-time and bring people along my healing journey to #couplegoals. Not because I wanted to be in love (I was just as freaked out by relationships as I was about being single) but because I felt this was my mission.

Now, before you think, "Not another relationship coach wannabe," let me explain. I always sensed that Love was important and that somehow it would be integral to my life (my grandmother's words had reminded me of that). I also had an inkling that I was here to spread it. I can't explain this knowing other than every time I think about it, my whole body tingles, and this weird smile appears on my face like I just met a newborn puppy. But in lieu of actually healing my Shit, fashioning my experiences into a phoenix-from-the-ashes story felt like an easier win.

It didn't matter that I was never going to help anyone with anything useful because I would have been recycling old-school rhetoric dressed up with new-age buzzwords. It didn't even matter that I would have been secretly relying on social media quotes to explain my feelings, horoscope apps for romance compatibility, and a well-thumbed copy of someone else's manipulation manual disguised as a self-help dating book. I needed a socially acceptable reason for my pain, and I needed a tangible purpose for my endurance.

That's why karma is the player that no one wants to play with, but it's the MVP. It connects to our power by pushing us to grow up. It doesn't make us believe we are not *good enough* to do so, it just ensures that something happens so that we can find all the ways that we aren't. And it's those reasons that we have to challenge. Karma may be messy and painful, and it may feel like a battle of life and death because we are killing all the barriers to understanding our power and then exercising it.

I'd gotten it all upside-down. I created a destination and asked someone else for directions, all the while telling everyone else it was my decision and explaining to them how I made it. When I think about it, I was looking for someone else to fulfill my life purpose, and I thought that was empowering… Well, it isn't just upside-down; I was as far away from my purpose as possible. No wonder I never got out of bed before 10am. My mind was exhausted trying to make that one make sense.

Purpose is what allows us to find our healing and divinity, but we are not our purpose, nor is it our identity. Rather, purpose is an expression of us that shifts and grows as we do; it always reflects who we are and what brings us joy. It doesn't serve us (or anyone, for that matter) to define ourselves by what we do and what we can provide to others. In fact, all it does is leave us straddling a narrow set of circumstances that we cannot free ourselves from.

By deciding that the first step on my "purpose journey" would be to find someone else, I made my whole purpose contingent on something outside of me—that is, only *when* I found someone could I start living my purpose. *If* I couldn't, then I would never complete it. It *must* be this way because that's how people before me had done it.

Don't Worry Baby

There is more to Love than just a good night, a good fuck, and a good connection. In *A Karmic Affair*, I explain that the four pillars of Trust form the foundation of Love.

1. Trust (the understanding that everything is for our highest good);
2. Faith (that some unseen force has our back);

3. Hope (the reflection of our heart's desires); and
4. Knowing (the instant recognition of a truth).

Love—that is, shining our light for everyone to see—is the most divine act we can do as humans. In exercising Love, we not only become whole, but we also dissolve the Separation and polarity within us. By exercising trust, faith, hope, and knowing, we are acting in Love. This enables us to transcend our karma and create our new world.

Love delivers us to our purpose and allows us to share that Love in everything that we do. Our purpose is not a prison, and it was never meant to be. It's how we learn what it takes to be happy (or even in bliss), and that starts with finding our light and sharing it. That is how we allow our purpose to become what it's meant to be.

Love and purpose can only come through us as they start from the inside and express out. They aren't dependent on someone or something else, nor do they have anything to do with the external at first. But in a society that is riddled with Separation, where everyone is, in some way or another, denying a part of themselves to gain favor with someone else (so much so that they often don't realize it), it's totally understandable that we assume our purposes are dependent on others. But unless we heal what keeps us separate on the inside, we will be in a revolving door with every other relationship we encounter, including the one with our purpose—until it isn't our purpose but an uncomfortable copyright issue.

I thought I'd figured it all out: my purpose was love, and someone else was going to help me find it, and I was going to teach it to everyone else. At least I was serving, which seemed to be the main takeaway.

Serving wasn't the main takeaway, though. In asking other people permission to be in Love by asking them to love me, I made my purpose a side note, as well as all the work I was doing to heal myself. I couldn't bring anything through me or express myself when I was worried about how that expression would be received. It seemed there was too much at stake that when I did meet someone, and it seemed to be going somewhere, I believed I needed them to stay connected to love. When our connection became more tenuous, either because of the pressure I put on the interaction or because we hit a bump in the road, so did my connection to love.

But if I was really honest with myself, when the connection dissipated (even if they were still in my life), I didn't miss them. Rather, I missed how I felt within that connection. I missed the light in the mirror that they were holding up to me. I missed feeling excited, desirable, happy, and beautiful. Most of all, I missed feeling alive. I had focused on someone else giving those feelings to me, but they were only reflecting it back to me. It wasn't a relationship with someone else I was looking for, it was the shining version of me.

My intuition wasn't wrong, but my expectations and explanations for how it would actualize in the physical world were too limited. Turns out the Love I'd been craving was how I shined when I was with them. I told myself that my purpose was being loved, not being in Love. And those are two very distinct things. So, when I applied that wisdom differently, namely following my heart, my mind expanded past the limitations I had created for myself.

By tapping into my own Love, I expressed it in everything I did, including my relationships. I poured my Love into my work with Liz so that it became an expression of me, I poured my Love into my other passions and pursuits, and I created a world that's filled with my Love—and that's all I see. It's how I found others who matched me, because as I expressed myself, I gave room for them to express themselves, too. Our Love gets deeper and our relationships get far better as a result.

We really cannot understand how much relationships define our lives until we make sense of our relationship with ourselves. We don't exist in a vacuum. No one, not even the hermit on the mountaintop, really lives in a bubble. The more conscious we become, the more we realize just how connected we are. It's that very connection that allows us to serve others, and it's through our purpose that we do so, because everything that we do gets laced in the Love we give it, so that light spreads even further until the world is filled with it. Moreover, the happier we are, the more we express joy and the more joyful our connections are.

Purpose was never meant to be about giving myself over to the collective, it was about giving my life back to me. In doing so, not only could I help others by showing up, but I could also keep learning more about who I was and what I wanted—so that I could offer more Love in the process.

Hold the Line
Liz

There's a Talmudic legend about how the philtrum came to be. It says that the Angel Lailah pressed that area gently so that babies would forget all the secrets of the universe. As romantic as it sounds, there's one very minuscule grain of truth. We are born with knowledge (aka divine connection), and we are compelled to forget it.

From an early age, I could see lights and Angels and Guides—not that I was aware of what I was doing. But I was clear that I needed the support of and a conscious relationship with the Divine to see me through my young years until I could get to the other side.

Experiencing the Divine is really difficult to put into words, but I'll try. When we're born with a level of consciousness where we see there is more to our existence than our daily grind, it can be a struggle. Straddling two worlds requires a lot of energy. Since this world isn't used to all that light, it makes life easier (not better) to forget, so we tend to opt for the path of least resistance, and that's where our suffering begins.

That's what I mean by the other side. I couldn't fully forget, but I couldn't hold it all, so I maintained just enough until I could burn out enough of my own angst and perceived suffering so I could remember again. And that was enough.

It may be easy to assume that psychics or mediums have different childhoods or must be special or so aware that they exist apart, but for most, we can't do what we've come here for if we can't truly live and understand what it means to really be human.

I don't just mean that "To live is to have loved," "To have loved is to have lost," or "To survive is to find meaning in our suffering," but we need to really be a real human without applying some spiritual context. We need to understand how fucking uncomfortable life on Earth is.

We've all hidden away parts of ourselves at some point in our lives. Maybe we were led to do so by well-intentioned parents who didn't want us to be teased or taunted by bullies. Perhaps a religious leader thought we were falling out in the eyes of their god. It could even be that we consciously hid ourselves, believing that there was no way we could be seen, let alone accepted for who we were. Often, that's how it begins. We assure ourselves it's for our own protection. It's just easier this way.

It often works for a while. The problem is, however, that we disappear along with the parts we've hidden. The longer we hide those parts of ourselves, the harder it becomes to reclaim what's good about them. That's the issue with keeping ourselves in the dark. The dark twists what was once light, and the longer those parts of ourselves remain hidden, the more twisted they become until we cannot recognize them anymore and struggle to reintegrate them.

Karma is the way to bring us out of the wasteland of Separation, to heal the Shit of that traumatic experience. But the polarity and judgment that underscores these experiences often hold us hostage to 3D longer than we care to admit. While it may be easy to blame this on our egos, it's also our relationship to our divinity that holds us back.

Souls cannot exist fully in Separation, which is to their detriment. This is why we have addiction. This is why we suffer. This is also why we're forced to disconnect from the Divine in the first place—to make it tolerable. As a result, the main tentpoles of 3D (religion, government, and financial institutions) become poor surrogates for the Divine, which is why we tend to worship through one of these.

Take It On the Run

Our perceived limitations based on our karmic stories show up in many ways, not just in our relationship with the Divine but in our relationships with ourselves and others. Whether it's a situationship we'd have preferred to be a relationship, a marriage of convenience rather than one filled with fun and passion, or denying ourselves the challenge of work that would excite us but settling for a job that didn't to be safe. But in settling for this sort of minimal love and listening to the *shoulds* instead of our desires, we have suffered and denied ourselves happiness.

Eventually, we figure out how to transcend our karma, but we have to know it inside out first. There's always a lesson or a reason, but it's often not what we expect. Our ability to grasp the lesson has everything to do with how honest we are with ourselves, and that honesty is determined by how fearless we are when faced with the ugly truth we've been avoiding.

It's one thing to know we're here for a reason, it's another to go through the painstaking process of figuring out or remembering that reason—or even more challenging, how to realize it. As I'd shared in a previous book, I knew that mine was spiritual. I didn't think that seeing Angels or speaking to Guidance was a plausible career path, but when I was nineteen and met the master teacher of Soul Memory Discovery, I found it. However, not having lived much of a life by then, I suspected it would have to wait.

In some twisted logic, I'm glad it did. I'm not a fan of the notion that good things come to those who wait. It only leaves us looking over our shoulders, wondering *if* it'll ever happen and whether we've proved ourselves worthy. Even though I was experiencing all the things I wanted to, I still questioned when the work would show up. (Remember, in *A Karmic Attraction*, I always say the *whens* and the *hows* are the biggest karmic bitches?) At times, I was frustrated, speculating on why I couldn't make my spiritual practice a bigger part of my daily life, blaming all my transcontinental moves, and thinking if only I'd had more time or space to make room.

Yet, deep down, I also knew I wouldn't really be like every other spiritual teacher I'd met. Goddess dresses aren't flattering on my small frame, cocoa ceremonies are lost on me, and while I like a pretty crystal just as much as the next person (Rhea has a nice collection), all that energy would make me light-headed.

I wouldn't have been able to figure out exactly the type of teacher I could be if I hadn't learned how to be me. I'll always remember one session I had with my teacher, Ellen; my Guides said I needed some cognitive knowledge first. What they were effectively saying was that I needed to grow up before I could understand my purpose and mission. What I was learning was far more valuable, which only came to me much later; every day that I was living and breathing as me was the best thing I could offer the world.

While I know that statement is more Rhea-style, she's not wrong. That's what's become lost when it comes to modern spirituality as it's shared today. The emphasis on what to wear, what supplements to take, what diet to follow, what retreats to take, and how many followers their healer has is merely spiritual cosplay. Absolutely none of those things speak to our actual divine connection. Rather, they keep us enslaved to the idea that there will always be more work to keep up our "spiritualness," thus moving us further from, not closer to, the Divine.

We are here to be the most human we can be and elevate that experience through spirituality without losing sight of the fact that it's all about keeping humanity intact. I was learning to embody exactly what I'd always known I'd come here to do, which was to live as me, fully connected, traversing the world, and remembering the Divine at every turn. So by the time I could get beyond full divinity to complete divine consciousness whereby my whole life was woven in Spirit, I wouldn't lose sight of what this whole consciousness game was about—bringing humanity and the Divine so close together that All can be regained (as in, the entirety of who we are collectively creates the All).

This is why we explore our karma piece by piece, relationship by relationship, and experience by experience, so that we don't become overwhelmed by this challenging process, which can take years and years to go through. (To be fair, it took Rhea roughly three years of concentrated daily work, while it took me around three decades.) Yet, freedom from 3D demands freedom from everything that we believe defines us, our lives, and how we live in Separation, which is why our very relationships with our work, personal relationships (family, dating, and partnership), and our faith have been under the microscope.

Everything is up for examination, no matter how small or inconsequential. We are contending with everything that we've taken for granted in 3D. Yet, it's through accepting this that we begin the final process of this revolution, which is living our purpose. Only when we are living our purpose will we ever root in Oneness.

For What It's Worth
Rhea

I believed that spirituality was an unexplored solution that would present me with my prize. I didn't want to accept my power or my knowing because I'd have to take responsibility for my choices. That's what appealed to me about this whole spirituality gig—I wanted someone else to tell me how great a job I was doing, how much progress I was making, and that I could have faith.

Faith can be a very strange word and a very uncomfortable concept. It often implies that there is something outside of us that is in control. But, as told in detail in *A Karmic Affair*, I learnt that I didn't need faith in anyone or anything else. I just needed to recognize how much faith I already had in myself.

I'd achieved so much, and I had been the One to make so much happen for me, but I still couldn't see that I was capable of having faith in myself. But it was only when I stepped back and connected the dots that I saw what was really going on: to live in Separation, I had to be separate too. I had to separate myself from the knowing that I was not only *good enough* to make my own choices but also *good enough* to create my joy. Even though I didn't realize my power, I was still exercising it—only without the consciousness to fully comprehend what was happening.

We choose to get ourselves out of our karma, we choose to find our power, and then we choose to step into our divinity. It's always been up to us. Sure, we can outsource our choices to someone else, but we are still letting them make those choices for us. That means that even when we surrender, we are choosing to surrender. But it's hard to take responsibility for our lives. It's even harder to accept that no one else can take responsibility for us.

I was the one who turned up at Liz's door. I was the one who said yes to being on that podcast. I was the one who stayed when it didn't deliver me what I thought I wanted. I was also the one who said no to staying in a job I hated, said yes to one who I loved, and kept saying yes every time a new opportunity that felt right presented itself to me. I may have said that I had no faith in myself, but I showed up every time. And when I did take a wrong turn, whatever that was, I knew pretty quickly that something had gone wrong.

We are always the most powerful people in our lives, and no god, guru, partner, or friend can ever fully take that away from us. We are always making the choice to listen to someone else, and we are always making the choice to give away our power when we believe it has been taken away. However, there is always another way, choice, and avenue we haven't explored, and the second we understand that is also the second we allow ourselves to conceive other choices.

When we decide based on a desired outcome rather than our consciousness, and it doesn't work, we can easily fall back on why we made that decision, second-guessing ourselves to the point of delusion and madness. This is because the pain and the conflict aren't in the outcome, they're in the decision itself.

I didn't care what the outcome was as much as I cared about the choice itself. What I couldn't grasp was that the two worlds I'd been living in weren't quite matching anymore. My internal world told me there was more to come, and it was still unfolding, but my external one wasn't changing fast enough, so I dismissed the idea that it was changing at all. Not because I believed I wasn't *good enough* to experience it but because I wasn't seeing how much of it I was already experiencing.

We have to understand that our best bet may not be the predictable choice that serves us the most; rather, it is the one we never saw coming but enriches us in ways we never believed possible. Sometimes, it's only obvious why much later down the line. Every step I took (even when I believed they were missteps) was perfect for me, and I knew what was best for my life, even if I tried to tell myself otherwise. It was bullshit to say that anyone could know more than me about my life and where it was going. I always had the freedom to be myself and shine my light.

When I understood that I could be the One to not only create my life but also create it the way that was best for me, I also understood how many choices were available. Once I recognized that I had always been whole, as me, I finally started creating the life that I truly desired, with no settling or exception. But I didn't have to plan and plot where I was heading, I just had to keep choosing and letting my life unfold.

I may have felt like I was helping others heal, but I couldn't shine the way when I was still searching for a flashlight. But by redefining my own ideas of what faith, spirituality, and my path needed to look like, I was shining. I may not have known everything, but I knew enough, and I always ended up saying, "I was right."

My Way

All the toxic behaviors, the self-flagellation, and the perpetuation of my unlovable story wasn't me. All the expectations I created about what my life needed to look like and what I needed to achieve by a certain age wasn't me either. They were strategies I had adopted to survive Separation, so I could feel like I was moving forward and growing up, even though I wasn't growing very much at all.

Except, as that power was being exercised in my destruction, I had to first take responsibility for my demise before I acknowledged that I could apply it differently. I hadn't been listening to what felt right to me, I was doing what I thought was right and then getting frustrated when it didn't turn out the way I'd envisaged it. But when I took back my power and engaged with the work from a conscious place as opposed to being its victim, I recognized that there were more options than I had previously assumed. In fact, I was already making headway by listening to myself, albeit in small doses. In freeing myself from the self-imposed trap that avoiding my fate kept me in, I availed myself of far more choices than I could have conceived of.

We can't get to our purpose when we are mired in what our purpose should be and what it can deliver to us. We also can't express it when we allow others to define it for us. Otherwise, we will end up waiting whilst sacrificing the very things that bring us joy—ensuring that we remain outside of our purpose.

If we know that something else is possible, but we refuse to acknowledge it for fear of making some dire mistake, we ensure that our past dictates our present and narrows the perception of our future. It can leave us feeling stuck because we can't see what difference we are striving for. What we don't often see is that our actions may be what is best for us, even if they don't always seem that way. No matter how we think we are self-sabotaging, we are also doing it for a reason. It will always make sense for us, even if it seems toxic or unhinged.

When I judged the validity of my feelings through the narrow lens of my expectations, I couldn't see how much my life had changed. My work had to evolve as I evolved, and my notion of revolutionary could grow as I did—until

I could see that it was possible to be in joy with whatever I engaged in, be it social, romantic, familial, career, or just a hobby that excited me. It wasn't about choosing the work or my experience of it wholesale, it was about choosing what worked for me.

But because I was exercising my power in a world where very few even understand what power can be (including myself), I looked out of control, felt out of control, and probably acted a little out of control—which was the point.

Being out of control meant that I wasn't letting anyone or anything control me. I wasn't listening to what had been done before and forcing myself to mimic that. Instead, I was finally listening to myself and honoring myself with corresponding actions. So, when I made a choice to follow my joy, no matter what came next, I couldn't regret it because I knew I wouldn't have chosen any other way.

Regardless of what happened as a result of my choices, the act of making them was where I exercised my power. I never could see where my choices would lead; all I could do was trust that they would be in my best interest, have faith that my desires would be realized, know that I could listen to myself, and hope that it would be better than I could have imagined. All I had to do was write my own rules, make my own choices, and let my life unfold—trusting that I could handle everything that came my way.

Heaven Must Have Sent You
Liz

We can't experience what it means to have a joyful and peaceful life until we really lose our Shit and heal it. That's really the point of ending Separation. But some want more and have always sensed there is more to their lives than their 3D reality. They may have often perceived or seen what is unseen by many. They may have known or believed in things without prompting. They may have understood esoteric principles or ideas without ever needing them put into words. They may have, like Rhea, shown up at my door (early for once in her life, I might add) because they knew they were here to do more than live an average existence.

Souls on a mission come into body with a specific contract. This contract merely states that they are here with a very specific intention: to support the transition from Separation into Oneness by enabling a particular knowledge, practice, healing, understanding, or teaching that only their being can express.

While it's possible to cancel mission contracts, given that we're the ones making them, it's very difficult. Mission contracts are like blood oaths, and there's so much riding on pummeling Separation to the ground in this particular lifetime that to break a mission contract, we'd have to really be unable to fulfill it, which is why there are so many out there whose sole purpose is to assist mission work.

That assistance may come with big social media platforms and followings. They've written books that get readers to consider what it means to become self-aware, meditate, and wrestle with their addictions and demons. They promote alternative ideas and healing work to open minds about what it means to live an elevated human experience as opposed to a Shitty experience.

While not all of their ideas work in the karmic realm and beyond, they've helped mainstream some form of spirituality (even if it's a bit airy-fairy or, worse, commodified), which has helped people shift their perspectives towards divinity. These influencers have paved the way for the lesser-known teachers who've held space for the Light for decades, the ones who are coming, or those who have yet to be born.

This Separation-to-Oneness process is long and requires hundreds of Earth years to become a reality, which means we're really at the beginning of the beginning of a new time. That's not to say we won't see massive headway in our lifetime. On the contrary, since this is the lifetime to end Separation, we'll witness the surfacing of all the Shit in need of healing and the coming of the ones to heal it. Every piece healed plants the seeds for future peace, so it requires particular souls with specific missions to usher in this age of Oneness. Without them, we'd easily lose our way.

The objective of any spiritual teacher is to become redundant. We're not here to create a legacy or a body of work that lasts for eternity. Nor are we here to become surrogates or substitutes for Spirit. All we can offer is a singular teaching and remind people of what they have forgotten: they and the Divine are One. That's really at the core of our pain, the fact that we've fallen short of our divinity time and again. We've compromised our desires for our perceived wants, we've undersold our worth for external validation, and we've hurt ourselves and others in the process.

Karma is inescapable. It will always be at our doorstep until we burn it out. But even then, we can push away, avoid, and rationalize the hell out of it. We can even turn it into a purpose, taking others on our healing journeys or our journeys through hell. We can claim we're victims while simultaneously contributing to our own victimhood. We've become so gifted at commodifying our issues and turning them into entertainment fodder for friends and followers that we may become less inclined to divest ourselves of our karma—not when it garners us so much attention, which our egos love. Validation is everyone's 3D success story.

It's often said that we are humans having a spiritual experience or spiritual beings having a human experience. As I said in *A Karmic Attraction*, however, our perspective is so often skewed by our karma and egos that we conflate our divinity by hiding our imperfections and insecurities behind a generic "spiritual" label.

We are souls who are here to make the most of being in body and facilitate the single most important objective of our lifetimes—to remember that we are not only divine but the Divine. We are doing all of this while in body and are conducting this vast experience of this consciousness game within specific physical and evolutionary limitations.

Yet, it's near impossible to recognize the Divine within and without when we're knee-deep in our Shit and karma, and the rest of the world is reflecting back the worst of our human existence. It makes it difficult to grasp that beneath all of our human detritus lies a core that is so beautiful and so divinely created that it perfects us.

Many of us have forgotten or are beginning to forget that the journey is a lifelong one. It's not indicative of a life of struggle, rather it's indicative of a life committed to ending struggle. We've become caught in a web that keeps us stuck in struggle without seeing the purpose of struggle has always been about emerging from it with wisdom and wholeness.

The reason we struggle, the reason for the fight, whatever it is, no matter how big or small, is the catalyst for our coming into wholeness on the other side—not to become celebrities or have a following that feeds our vanity or to even change people's lives. We're here to point the way, to sow a single seed of Love that might transform a person's life when they're ready.

Heaven Help

I have written about the various periods of consciousness throughout our recent history that have been intended to spare humanity its untimely self-destruction. These periods of consciousness are assisted by those souls whose primary directive is to shape the collective consciousness moving towards enough divine consciousness that humanity can see beyond its inherent need for survival and work towards a more collaborative way of being.

Naturally, progress on a large scale requires a few lifetimes and generations before we can see any meaningful change, and because Separation consciousness is so dense, it just takes more time than many of us would prefer. This is why we had our largest swath of souls arrive in the 1970s, those beings who would stop at nothing to get us to examine our choices to remain separate in a world that could no longer support it. In the path of these bold ones have followed more souls whose primary directive has been focused on seed planting, while those generations since 2006 came in for world-building.

When we read terms such as "foundations" and "world-building," we may look outside our windows and wonder what's changed. The reality is that change was never going to be global or even communal until we burned out the main reason for keeping us at war with each other, which is the Separation within. Until then, these souls could do their best to hold every piece of God consciousness contained within them with the sole intention of bringing it forward once the world could support their contribution.

Starseeds is the designation of a soul whose primary mission (or directive, for Star Trek geeks out there) is to assist in raising the consciousness of Earth and her beings, from that of Separation to Oneness. There are not many of them in body at present, and certainly not as many as is believed.

These particular souls are here to be in service to their mission, which for some is establishing God consciousness on this Earth plane. They occupy all walks of life with the primary purpose of planting seeds for harmony and cooperation in all the 3D tentpoles so we have a foundation for Oneness. These souls have two unique features that are not shared by non-Starseed souls:

1. Their mission is directly tied to their planet of origin. So, depending on where the soul originated, the features of that planet and star system will be expressed by the soul.

2. They will vibrate higher than non-Starseeds, so living in Separation is a much bigger struggle for them than the average soul. They may naturally gravitate towards various coping mechanisms to make the energy more bearable (Addiction City, here we come), seek to live away from crowded places, be surrounded by animals or pets to help ground the energy around them, go to extreme

lengths to hold on to their "star" selves which may make them seem super "out there," or become part of extreme movements that seek to destroy Separation, whatever the cost.

While some may associate with the idea of Starseeds, it doesn't necessarily mean that they are Starseeds. It could be that they had experienced a lifetime (in a spiritual sense, a lifetime is not the same as a human life span) or more somewhere else (a bit like taking a vacation), but it's not indicative of their soul origin.

Starseeds are not to be confused with Aliens (nor do they share any alien DNA), although they may show a predilection for them because they long for a sense of home that is beyond Earth's energy. To be clear, Starseeds are completely and utterly distinct from Aliens for a couple of reasons, the first and most important one being karma. Starseeds can carry karma, while Aliens cannot. They do so because incarnating in this lifetime in Separation allows them to divest themselves of their karma while in service to their mission. They get a twofer, which is spiritual pragmatism at its best.

Yet, these souls don't come from the heavens, despite their moniker, "Starseeds." Even if their qualities are attributed to planets or star systems, if we consider the vast universe that is a part of all of our beings, given that we are all emanations of the Divine, then we are all Starseeds. It's a little meaningless and doesn't speak to the unique features of the soul and its purpose. It's just that these particular souls are that much more connected to their divinity, to their divine knowing and connection, that they are really the embodiment of the Divine.

Aliens, on the other hand, are beings who carry more Source DNA than other souls. Source DNA is quite simply encoding for full divine presence (this is not to be confused with Angels who are not souls but rather expressions of Source and, therefore, more divine). In human form, Aliens are essentially enrobed in the Divine, so they do not share the same consciousness as most people and thus do not carry karma, nor do they hold any Separation or even Oneness. Their consciousness extends beyond dimension and space. As a result, they may come off as otherworldly or capable of more than the average amazing person and will tend to lead unconventional lives. Of course, they might have human experiences, some disappointments, and feel pleasure, but their extreme level of detachment from the rest of humanity may make them seem more robotic than human.

This is solely because they are not here for a human experience. Rather, they are here to establish a framework for whatever consciousness will enable human evolution. They may not be fully aware of it, but they are firmly directed and purpose-driven. Souls on a mission, on the other hand, are responsible for establishing that consciousness within the particular systems Aliens create. These Aliens have been working on this framework for the past forty years and will continue to do so for the next several generations to help humanity operate in Oneness.

Their Source DNA (aka divine presence), coupled with the tremendous work they do throughout a variety of industries, means they tend to stand out to garner trust and faith from those souls who so badly seek the new consciousness that they are here to enable. There's a catch, however. Humans are never perfect, and that has always been the point of being human—to get comfortable with our imperfections. Aliens, given their one-track purpose, often act with impunity and seem untouchable because of their high level of intelligence and gifts.

They have a job to do, and that is it. But so long as they are in body, they are not infallible. Their fallibility rests in the fact that they do not really connect to human emotional complexities, and as a result, if they are too mission-focused, their ideology can blind them to the point that they miss the overall picture of what they are trying to achieve and hurt people along the way. This can lead to massive disappointment and disillusionment among their fans and followers, of which there are often many.

Between Aliens and Starseeds, it may seem that humanity would have enough help. Except there's karma, that inescapable nagging bitch that will linger as long as Separation hangs around. As a result, there will be souls in service to 3D until it no longer serves anyone's growth and evolution. Earth and its capacity to hold Separation is a great playground for any soul that wants to play in these energies. Once there is enough critical mass for 5D to become global, Earth will no longer be in service to 3D.

But some souls are here for this 3D-to-5D, Separation-to-Oneness leap who don't have a mission. Their planet of origin may be Earth or some other dimension. They could be souls who offer their assistance by merely holding space for the consciousness upgrade. They are here for the whole vast Earth experience that is ripe with opportunities for growth and evolution, but they are not guided by a specific purpose—except to be the best souls they can be. It's a bit like being the host of a party. They, along with Starseeds and Aliens, are making the space ready by preparing the décor and adding some lovely, high-vibratory aesthetic, but the life of the party is the people who show up.

And there are people showing up. They come from all places and spaces, bringing diverse energy, experiences, and wisdom to the party. These souls, who are neither on a mission nor Aliens, are pretty great. What makes them distinct and deserving of this consciousness rave is the level of commitment they have shown to humanity over the ages. They have survived plagues, the fall of empires, the destruction of nations, fought wars, died in battles, and been conquered all in the name of Separation. They have played, and continue to play, in this Earth's game for lifetimes to make whole this experiment of the Divine.

Good Vibrations
Rhea

My story about searching for Spirit had never been about whether I felt it. It was about whether I could explain it and listen to it. In fact, for a time I was somewhat of a professional dabbler—I'd seen crystal healers and a handful of psychics, and I'd even done a past life regression. Those sessions echoed what I already felt but couldn't put into words and offered me a degree of hope that I had been struggling to find by myself.

My problem was that when I felt the goosebumps, the peace, or even the knowing that I was protected, I dismissed it all because there was nothing or no one to tell me it was real. I didn't trust myself to believe what I was experiencing, and I didn't want to put my faith in the inkling that told me that things were going to turn out better than what I could see. That felt too risky, too dangerous, and too much like a death wish.

I searched high and low for answers, reading every book I could get my hands on and speaking to everyone who seemed to have a modicum of wisdom (it's quite astounding what one can achieve when they are impatient and highly motivated). I wanted to believe in what I felt, but going to every person to explain my feelings, I didn't get very far. My mind kept trying to prove that I was wrong and stuck me in a loop of self-sabotage—until it got to the point where none of it made sense.

That's the thing about going to others for the answers. They just can't give them to us. We always filter what they say through the limits of our minds and translate them through our expectations. Since those outcomes are usually a way to relieve ourselves from the fear that we are not *good enough* and avoid that fear, we do not pursue what we really want.

We may have all the tools to facilitate our power, but we take that Separation outside and bring it in. What we don't realize is that in doing so, we end up cutting off a huge part of who we are and what we can achieve. We can't be our true selves, we deny our desires, and we tell ourselves that we can't achieve them with ease.

That is what fear creates and what the ego perpetuates. We are confined to what we know and what we can expect, and as it's pretty Shit, we end up trying to avoid it at the same time. Yet, the more we try to evidence our feelings, the more we allow our minds to dilute them and doubt them. We create stories that don't exist, we conflate our role within them, and we allow our fears and ego to take hold of the reins—all the while telling ourselves that unless our reasoning or knowing is bulletproof, it is of no use to us.

While operating from my mind, I made everything conditional on my expectations of the result whilst not believing the result could be joyful. For instance, my dating life was Shit because I was looking to anyone to validate I was *good enough*. So I continuously landed myself in Shit whilst running away from Shit and lamenting that everything smelled a bit Shitty. And, when the outcome didn't quite align with the Shit I had come to expect, I twisted it to look Shitty anyway because my mind couldn't conceive that it could be any other way—creating self-fulfilling prophecies every time I swiped right.

But we are often taught to rely on our minds over our feelings. We explain everything in precise detail (and when I say *explain*, I mean have infallible reasoning, method, and results) to show how it came about. We treat a beneficial result of acting on a feeling as magical, whilst we treat a beneficial result of acting on a thought as assured—without ever questioning whether it could be the other way around. There is no room for surprise, and there is no room for actual growth. There is no room for the unknown to have credibility, and there is no room for the unexplainable to have merit.

Spirituality isn't a route to our divinity the way most people perceive it. It's not about lighting some sage, doing some visualizations, and hoping that as we manipulate our energy, our world will follow suit. Spirituality cannot be a coping mechanism for our Shit or a way to show that we don't have Shit in the first place. It also can't be an excuse for our powerlessness or to prove we are a perpetual victim. To grow up is to own our power, not sublimate it. It's our light, and we decide how to express it.

I wasn't asking for guidance, I was asking for permission. But all anyone could do was show me where I doubted myself and what I was creating as a result. If I couldn't trust myself, then I wouldn't trust anything, no matter how sweet it appeared. And until I could accept that I didn't want to play in Shit, regardless of where it was coming from, I would be stuck in it.

Come Home To Me

I remember the first time I met my Guides. It was November 2018, and I was sitting on Liz's couch, unsure what the fuck was happening. Liz communicates with them through a pendulum, but being a medium, she can also hear them. So, obviously, I was skeptical. I wasn't sure I believed in the Guides, and I wasn't convinced she wasn't the one moving her hand emphatically. But, as I said in a previous book, I also felt that it wasn't Shit, either. As I listened to Liz connecting with the wisdom of something bigger than both of us, my heart began to open again.

To be fair, if I were looking for corroboration for my experiences, there are loads of books and accounts of spirits, Angels, Master Guides, regular Guides, the list goes on. Not everyone could be wrong. But the session with Liz allowed me to do something that I hadn't dared to do for a very long time: to open myself up to a feeling I had long been holding back.

Problem was, I turned Liz into a one-stop psychic shop that could predict my future, and every time she said something that made me uncomfortable (which was more often than I would have liked), I internalized it to the point that it was gospel. As a result, I started fearing Guidance and was nervous every time I asked a question despite being unable to stop asking at every turn. "It's my life," I wanted to scream, whilst turning to them to ask, "It is… right?"

Everything I engaged with became just as distorted as my self-perception. All I knew was a series of disappointments that I had projected onto Guidance. I was effectively forcing them to make up for all the disappointment by delivering a different life. But in doing so, they disappointed me too, and I recreated that toxic relationship with them that I had with everything and everyone else.

I couldn't get an answer that made sense to me since I didn't understand the disconnect between who I thought myself to be and what I wanted. Yes, I got a version of the answer that was never a lie, but because I only had one focus in mind (safety from further pain and disappointment), I was looking for an impossible binary answer. I may have thought that I was asking what would happen next, what the lesson was, if that person was significant, or what my next career move was, but I was asking to listen to myself. No one could answer that but me.

But here's the rub: some of what was said was literally a mirror to my fears, not the truth. And if that stood in the way of my karma-free life, Guidance would show me that time and time again. I was being forced to confront how powerless I believed myself to be so that I could finally get sick of it. I couldn't trust the Guides because I couldn't trust myself, so all they were doing time and again when I went to them was holding up a mirror to that fact. I didn't have faith in myself, so all they were showing me was that message cloaked in different answers.

That wasn't because the Guides couldn't know but because it was never up to them. I had so much more agency than I wanted to believe, but I couldn't relax because I didn't believe I could handle it. The Guides were doing everything in my best interest, but because I didn't want to grow up and own that power, their hands were tied as much as mine. I was always going to face the fact that I wasn't free until I freed myself.

Once we take that step back and truly understand that we have a choice, we start to grasp just how big those choices are and their impact. No one could tell me whether I would be hurt from an experience other than me. Not because I was in control of the hurt itself but because the more I was waiting to be hurt, the more I made it so by believing it was the only possibility.

That's why I was so pleasantly surprised when I started following my heart. Here was a method that required fewer thought calories but worked out so much better. It was a no-brainer (literally) that allowed me to finally find some peace and showed me there were no rules. Sure, it may have been challenging and required courage I didn't know I had, but that was the point all along: to see what I was capable of and how much joy and Love I could fill my life with.

I didn't plan, run through all the lists of pros and cons, and then slowly step whilst looking behind me. I jumped because it felt right. Every time I landed somewhere new, I allowed my mind to see how special those feelings were and what they could do for me—not the other way around.

I wouldn't get the guidance I craved until I figured out that I wasn't here to ask someone else how to live my life. My karmic undoing process is evidence of that, from first saying the words "Fuck This" to learning how to come into Love and realizing my purpose in the process. That new world I so craved was living inside me first; all I had to do was bring it into my physical reality by believing it was possible.

It may have been easier to focus on the bad and how Guidance hurt me by not telling me exactly what would happen and when, but even if they had told me, I wouldn't have believed it. I just wouldn't have got there because my mind was locked into what I thought it should look like. In allowing me to prove them wrong, they gave me the space to prove my knowing right, and that was a far bigger gift than my karma gave me. Not only did I see how powerful I was, but I also saw how to access and wield that power.

Initially, that looked like not speaking to Guidance at all (in fact, I didn't have a session with Liz for about two years), but the more I came into a peaceful and trusting relationship with myself and accepted that I was my own guide first and foremost, the more I expanded that into all my relationships, including the one with Guidance.

You're Not Alone
Liz

We may wonder why we are still dragging ourselves through our stories personally and globally—and, as a result, why 5D Oneness just seems to be a much further goal than we once perceived. Yet, no being can really move from one form of consciousness to another, let alone from Separation to Oneness, without first realizing their divine identity. Doing that allows them to shed the part of themselves that believes they and God are not the same (the very root of Separation).

This does not happen overnight. Part of the challenge of dismantling 3D while we are in body, in this lifetime, is we cannot dismantle ourselves all at once. We have to go bit by bit, piece by piece, to retain our sanity and some semblance of life.

Our Guides are the ones who are facilitating this new consciousness. They are contracted to help us realize our full divine identities, which we could never do before because of Separation. Unlike some Angels and demons, whose purpose is to serve our 3D experience, Guidance is here specifically for our 3D to 5D leap. In hierarchical order, our Guides are:

1. Archangels: Emissaries of the Divine who assist us in carrying out our purpose and mission. They also hold distinct features of the Divine.
2. Angels: God's messengers.
3. Divinities/Deities: Such as gods and goddesses.
4. Devas: Designers of our physical world.
5. Ascended Masters: Great beings who were once present in human form.
6. Guardian Angels: Those who protect and safeguard our physical well-being.
7. Guides and Animal Guides: Those we may have known during our lifetimes who serve as guides. In the case of animals, they may also be those beings who hold divine energy for us.

There are subcategories of each one of these (except the Archangels, who number at twelve), along with names, origins, histories, and lore that would fill several books. Guides are quite simply representatives of Source and carry with them the divine imprint and energy of the Divine. We may not have many, just enough to aid our evolution.

When any of these Guides serve on our Guidance Council, their imprint and energy are compatible with ours, and the guidance they provide is wholly aligned with our purpose and mission. It's precisely because we require different kinds of help that we may have different types of Guides. It would be near impossible not to have some because we need all the help we can get. But our relationship with them will differ depending on how we choose to live.

Our Guides play a slightly different role or present themselves in a way that makes them more compatible with and more easily identifiable to us. We are not born with our own Guides, but rather the ones our parents have. Eventually, as we energetically separate from our parents, around the age of seventeen (although it can be earlier), we usually get a few of our own to see us through life.

Pretty much everyone has a few Guides to aid in the move towards Oneness. How many we have hinges largely on our purpose and whether we're on a mission. Moreover, it depends on just how divinely focused our lives are intended to be. Frankly, if the goal is to be grounded and experience our humanity to the fullest extent possible, having a handful of Guides is more than enough. In this case, we just want the most kick-ass human life possible.

5D requires us to keep up that essential connection to our souls (a connection that can be hampered by our karma) to maintain the Oneness consciousness. This means raising our consciousness with every step we take towards our divinity. Guidance is just another piece of the larger puzzle of our fate that we are here to put together.

Guidance exists as a hierarchy. While it seems counter-intuitive, considering the end of 3D Separation is a dismantling of hierarchies, this exists for two reasons:

1. Vibration.

The higher the vibration, the stronger the Guide. This means that when we are connecting to a particular Guide (whether through meditation, free writing, or card readings), that vibration will speak to what we need to address, as in where we are holding our issue. Some Guides identify and illuminate issues in our physical and mental bodies but do not heal us on an emotional and spiritual level. Those are left to the Guides whose role is to bring us to a new understanding that allows for that information to unfold.

2. Consciousness.

We don't yet see ourselves as the divine beings we are. We are so preoccupied with the dregs of our human experience that we're not at a place in our consciousness to grasp that we are the Divine. It not only takes being in Oneness consciousness to do so but to expand our perception of who we are and the role we play in humanity's evolution.

Beyond The Invisible

It might take a village to raise a child, but it takes a host of divine energies and entities to usher humanity into a new consciousness. Since this consciousness is about Oneness and the Divine, humankind needs to reconnect with its own divine identity. Until we understand that we are the Divine at work, which means that we are just as powerful as any other being sourced from the Divine, we will see all other beings and entities as stronger, smarter, faster, and more gifted than us.

It's critical to understand vibrations because we often think that whatever we might be hearing or experiencing is from a higher source, but the reality is that unless we can attune to particular vibrations, most of us can't tell the difference between the Archangels, Angels, Ascended Masters, an earthbound spirit, or perhaps something less than divine.

Few people can attune themselves to the Guides' particular vibrations because it requires having divested ourselves of all fear, karma, and ego, *as well as* having a mission that such a gift serves the collective. Not everyone will want a conscious relationship with them, which may be too distracting or uncomfortable. Others may crave them in order to be awash with Light, to the point that they develop a co-dependence, but their Guides may not be as available to them as they prefer. What matters, ultimately, is that no matter who we are, we are not alone.

What we require more than anything is an expanded understanding of faith to see how Guides fit within the bigger picture of our lives. It doesn't matter how many we have. Numbers speak to nothing except what we require to best support our lives on Earth. What matters is acknowledging that we can begin to grasp that having Guides is how we bring Spirit to our everyday lives and infuse it with the Divine.

If our purpose or mission is tied to moving our consciousness from 3D to 5D, we require a ton more support to manage that transition. If, on the other hand, we are very much 5D beings in our wisdom and pursuit of purpose yet have our karma or other issues to contend with, our Guides will support us in maintaining our Oneness while divesting ourselves of our 3D Shit. Either way, Guidance helps us where we are unable to help ourselves, due to our fuzzy connection to our own divinity and life on Earth.

Our Guides are not part of our divine plan. That is, in the grand scheme of this consciousness game, they are not necessary or needed in the way many think. It may sound odd coming from us, where we talk about Guidance a lot in our podcast, but we do so because we understand what it takes. We're not channeling, we're not just speaking, and we're not just receiving—we're fully communing. Trust me when I say it isn't easy, and frankly, not everyone can do it. And that's okay. Consciousness isn't a pissing contest over who can predict the most accurate future or best see what your aura is. Consciousness is knowing the most profound truth to our very core, owning it completely, and living it every fucking day on this planet that is rife with Separation.

While our Guides are incredibly helpful when it comes to our evolutionary leap, they are not here to be us, nor are we meant to be a vehicle for them. Consider them consultants, if you will; they are useful until they've outlived their usefulness, which is when we are empowered enough to live according to our own divine will. If we're fearless enough to the point that we can embrace all the detritus of our lives and keep going, we see that we never really needed them in the first place. Hence, they are not part of our divine plan. We'd be here regardless and moving along our growth and evolution spectrum without them.

But they're not failing us. There are layers upon layers of consciousness, which means there are layers upon layers of how we see our Guides and the consciousness we choose to hold around them. What matters most is to know that we are truly supported by these divine beings who want this move into Oneness for humanity just as much as we do.

How Will I Know
Rhea

I have spoken a lot about how I met Liz and how, through the work, we created a manual for empowerment laced with the important lessons I learnt along the way. I have also touched on my fraught relationship with Guidance and how I used them as a crutch and a scapegoat for my powerlessness. What I haven't explained, as someone who is in a unique position to do so, is how to work with them rather than against them.

For a very long time, I wasn't even certain that they were another symptom of my unicorns-and-rainbows approach to life. That wasn't because I didn't want them to be true, although when I was steeped in my karmic story, they always seemed to be more Debbie Downer than cheerleader, so I kind of didn't want them to be true. It was because when I couldn't prove my experience of feeling them. I wondered whether they were real or just a figment of a wild imagination.

Sure, I'd heard them myself, and after sitting in a tiny closet for hours with Liz, I would have almost told you with complete certainty that she hears them too (her voice and tone change dramatically, which is always a little weird, but I'm used to it now). But I would always doubt them when I doubted myself. Until I could grasp my true power, I would be looking to prove they didn't exist.

Double-edged relationships were my thing in my karma, and my relationship with Guidance was no different. I wanted the shortcuts and the useful information, but because I didn't trust myself, I couldn't trust them either. What I couldn't appreciate at the time was that to work with Guidance in a way that served me, I needed to stop seeing them as other than me.

Separation has shaped us to believe that someone outside of us always knows better. We are also shaped to believe that if we found those answers ourselves, they would involve hardship, grueling lessons, and a revelation that may be sweet but not really worth the Shit we went through to get there. No wonder we look to others for shortcuts out of our pain and for the wisdom that eludes us.

However, we've become so used to outsourcing our experiences and wisdom by looking for someone or something else to explain or excuse our perceived failings. We buy the poison because we are convinced that we need some kind of antidote to the misery of our lives, without realizing that we aren't doing anything other than making ourselves sicker. We listen to self-proclaimed monks and gurus who believe they have the answers to what ails us when they don't even understand who we really are, and then we double down on their misguided bullshit (disguised as expertise) whilst wondering why things aren't getting fundamentally better or are only getting better for a short period.

It's not up to the Guides, some manifestation whisperer, or even our favorite chart reading to tell us what's going to happen in our lives and how to respond to it. They cannot fix us, our relationships, or our problems. They never could. But if we impose our own misunderstandings of our divinity onto them—whether it's assuming we cannot influence our lives to such a high degree (so we ask a million specific questions) or by fearing that good things come at a price (so we seek reassurance that things won't go tits up)—we will corrupt the interaction until we are resentful or despondent.

Guidance told me what was standing in the way of all the things that I desired (spoiler alert: it was me). When every question I asked was about how to be in my power, every answer showed me where I was giving it away. They weren't there to dictate what happened in my life and with whom—that was up to me. Moreover, despite the many ways I asked a question, the answer was never straightforward. There were always nuances and understandings that would never have made sense because my mind was too narrow. By the time their words made sense, I had already moved on to the next question.

I couldn't see that the answers I was receiving were offering another piece of information about what I wanted, what I desired, and how I was going to make it work. I also couldn't see that not only was the life I wanted best suited for me, but also that I was the One to create everything that brought me joy. But the reason that I couldn't see any of that was because I wasn't willing to take responsibility for my life. I didn't want everything blowing up on my watch, I wanted someone else to take the blame. I also didn't know what I would do when I had everything I wanted, as I wasn't convinced I could stand to lose it.

I stopped feeling let down by them when I accepted how powerful I really was. That's when I could ask for guidance and know that I could make my own choices regardless of what they advised. They were in my life to keep me moving on a forward trajectory, and yes, often their answers were prophetic, but not always in the way I expected.

For example, in my first session with Liz, they said that I was there for faith. I was, but I was there to learn what faith meant, what it facilitated, how it came from the inside of me, and how it was the leap to everything I ever wanted. I didn't understand that at the time. I thought they meant faith in something larger than me that knew better than me. But as I worked through my karmic Shit, I realized I was the only one who could figure out how to live my life and what to do with it. I also came to understand what faith really was and what it laid the foundation for.

Can You Feel It

It's easy to look back at the work and know that everything happened for a reason. If I hadn't learnt what I needed to uncover what I already knew, then I wouldn't have experienced true freedom. But when I remember how hard it was to face all the corners of myself, it still gives me pause because I know what it means to leave Separation completely. It's an undertaking unlike any other.

Spirituality takes a lot out of a person. Just when one thinks they've reached the top of the mountain, enlightenment, nirvana, or whatever end has been promised, there's more—whether it's our first "Fuck This" moment, facing our karma and fears (and eventually becoming karmaless and fearless), healing our three bodies (emotional, physical, and mental) so that we can become conscious, or killing the ego and integrating the spiritual body to reach higher consciousness. It requires a degree of conviction that most have never asked of themselves. So we tell ourselves that life sucks until we die, and we may as well lose ourselves in a slew of coping mechanisms until we do.

We approach spirituality no differently. We want to know how to get the guy, how to get the girl back, what job to take, or why we didn't manage to make the last one work. All we are doing is reinforcing the lie that we don't know or can't determine what's best for us. We further separate from our power and create the perfect storm to trick ourselves into believing we never had any. But true spirituality is not here to deliver us a dream life. It cannot.

We may come across a social media post that brings us relief, but it's our job to ask why or to act on it and find out. A friend marching us to an astrology session may reignite a feeling that there is something bigger out there, but that is only because we already feel there is. A retrograde, conjunction, or birth chart may tell us something about ourselves, but unless we have a feeling towards that aspect of ourselves, it won't mean anything.

Nothing means anything unless we ascribe our own meaning to it. Whether we blame our looks, our partner, the government, God, or a mysterious cabal, it doesn't matter. Whether we throw a thousand excuses as to why we are powerless and why it's hard to become powerful, it doesn't matter. It's only when we own ourselves and come to know ourselves, being ourselves whilst redefining what *ourselves* even means, that the world looks like the scenery, not the plot.

The moments I could act for myself were the moments I understood that. As I further connected to myself and expanded past my perceived limitations, I finally used spirituality as a tool as opposed to a salve that never healed anything meaningfully. My issues weren't going away until I faced them head-on, my fears weren't going to dissipate until I walked through them, and my life would never be mine until I owned it.

We're not here to become spiritual beings who forget their humanness; rather, we are here to elevate the human experience beyond what we've known it to be. Our spiritual path is about getting the most out of our lives. No one can give that to us, no matter how much we wish they could or how much they promise they know our secret. It is up to us. Everything else we buy into, regardless of how smart or couched in armchair wisdom it is, is just showing us where we still don't believe that and why.

That was the gift that Guidance gave me—they turned me back to myself at every question—so that no one but me could take credit for creating the life I desired. It also freed me because I didn't need them to facilitate it for me. That's why I don't regret asking the questions in the first place. If it wasn't for every one of those questions, I wouldn't have unlocked all the wisdom that allowed me to create the life I have now.

Don't get me wrong, when I tried to get the cheat sheet and shortcut through the painful parts, Guidance's input was invaluable. They offered a perspective that I may not have grasped because I was too close to something, a piece of information that unlocked a different approach, or some advice that was the exact thing I needed to hear at the ideal time. But even though they may have said something that opened my mind, when push came to shove, I was the One to listen to my heart, and I was the One who followed it to the next opportunity.

The pivotal moments of my karmic undoing process had very little to do with Guidance. It was always me who would bring that Love into my reality and always me who would experience it. That is the gift that keeps on giving because the connection I developed with myself is the source of my power.

Our happiness cannot be experienced like everyone else's, no matter how much the data tells us it can. We are our own beings with our own desires and our own ways of expressing them. We cannot optimize our lives by following a simple routine or drinking the elixirs created by someone else, nor can we conjure our dreams by reciting someone else's words.

Spirituality, as it is currently used, is a tool that will one day become obsolete. It cannot remain in its current iteration if we are to understand how powerful we can be and the immutable force of our divine connection. When we get there, there's no room for spirituality anymore, especially if it takes up space that could be otherwise taken up by things that are fun and bring a smile to our faces. As our lives become filled with joyful moments and meaningful relationships, we don't need to seek out a divine connection to reassure ourselves that it exists—we just know it.

Another One Bites The Dust
Liz

There is much more to who we are than our physical selves. The greater our consciousness, the more aware we become of how our mental and emotional bodies function. When we reach full consciousness, our spiritual body enters the equation; that's when we are in divine or higher consciousness, whereby all we are, see, hear, and do is in line with the Divine.

Our fate is all the unique ways we serve as the Divine and is underpinned by five divine values.

1. Happiness.

Happiness is born from two things. The first is that we are in full flow with our fate, living as the Divine in the most divinely human way possible. This may sound quite lofty, but it simply means that we are living our utmost desires while in full alignment with our purpose. The second is that we are recognizing our connection to others, and in that recognition, we can see ourselves in everyone. Being a part of this All brings us to a whole new understanding of Oneness, and when we realize it fully in our beings through our daily lives, we cannot be anything other than happy.

2. Trust.

In the previous books of this series, we have shared that the four pillars of Trust (trust, faith, hope, knowing) form the foundations of Love, which is one of the most critical pieces in the formation of our 5D world. As a divine value, Trust enables the I/Thou relationship that underpins 5D. I Am the Divine, and as the Divine, I recognize my full self in you. It's through this self-recognition that we experience pure, unadulterated trust that you will treat me as I treat you because we are the same at our core.

3. Humility.

Humility is accepting that we may not have all the answers or know what's best for ourselves or others, despite our best efforts. We struggle with humility in 3D because our egos often need to have all the answers (or the last word) to prove our worth, so the ego often masks it as disingenuous sincerity or magnanimity. Without the ego, humility gives space for others to contribute and show up as their unique selves while giving ourselves room to do the same.

4. Sharing.

Lack shapes our human experience. The belief that not only is there not enough but that there can never be enough for everyone has underpinned our 3D experience and how we treat one another. Sharing is a divine value because the more we share, the more we create (that is, as we give to others, we make room to create more). It's not karmic payback; rather, it's simple energy.

5. Harmony.

Finding harmony with others isn't possible in Separation because we are more skilled at focusing on our differences. Living in Otherness has shaped how we approach our relationships and keeps everyone at arm's length. Yet, when we heal our internal Separation and come into our fates, that flow is how we harmonize with the challenges that being alive in this world brings. As a divine value, harmony keeps us in flow with ourselves and with others because we understand that we are all part of this shared consciousness story.

We may exercise one or two of these divine values within our own families, relationships, and communities. By burning out our fears and divesting ourselves of our karma and ego identities, we could truly be happy, trustworthy, humble, generous, and harmonious. However, to express all five of these values requires something that we haven't yet reached but are well on our way to reaching, thanks to courage, and that is conviction.

In 3D, conviction is an expression of polarity, a belief that for every wrong, there is a right, and that for every problem, a solution can be found to bring about a sense of justice or equanimity. While that approach keeps people in line or serves the disadvantaged in 3D, it cannot work in 5D because Oneness negates polarity. Instead, like anything else that comes from 3D, it will have to shift to become part of our 5D consciousness.

This requires that we transform how we approach our notions of justice. Justice is not a divine value because we attach a sense of fairness to it, which makes it too subjective to exist in Oneness. Conviction in 5D is justice redefined. It's not based on fairness (again, too subjective) or right and wrong. Rather, it's based on the five divine values being exercised at once, which are enabled through courage.

It is likely that we won't see this kind of conviction exercised in our lifetime, and it will likely be left for our children's children to see it rooted in their society and experience. We have far too much 3D Separation to contend with and too many generations who carry the trauma of injustice and polarity. We can hope that they will heal it all while in body, but it's not yet certain.

We look to assuage our own pain when it comes to matters that affect and offend us. There is no way that justice could ever be enacted fairly or objectively when we hold so much pain and are shaped by our own suffering. As a result, we've been left with a sense that not only is life unfair but that it will never be fair.

When we struggle with notions of unfairness or victimhood, we know the ego isn't too far behind. This is for three reasons:

1. Fear.

The ego feeds off fear. Even if we're not holding any fear but those in our households, communities, governing bodies, and positions of influence over our well-being and autonomy are in fear, they will use the ego to navigate them to perceived safety, which is ultimately more of the same with bouts of emotional or mental relief.

2. Shame.

The ego loves shame because even if we know we are *good enough*, the residual doubts can easily become magnified when we have nothing in front of us to prove the ego wrong, which makes us feel even more groundless.

3. Blame.

We are not a collective of empowered individuals. We are, instead, a collective of victims, each stuck in their own victim story and unwilling to take responsibility or display accountability for their role in their story. Even when we claim responsibility, we often don't succeed because we cannot really understand why it all happened in the first place (FYI, it was the karma we created). Our inability to make karma *our* bitch keeps us karma's bitch.

All Right Now

The ego feeding off fear, reinforcing shame, and manipulating through blame became unleashed as this collective 3D experience began its long, slow unraveling to reach its final end. What was once the small voice that navigated our individual lives has taken on a life of its own. It's called cancel culture. While it's nothing new, and there are certainly old practices of shunning and shaming that predate it, modern cancel culture is vastly more dangerous and difficult to contend with because:

1. It negates individual thought, will, autonomy, and purpose.
2. It assumes that no one is capable of coming into Oneness on their own.
3. It forces collusion, groupthink, and ignorance.

Everything about modern cancel culture runs against the principles of 5D, which creates a tension between *intention* and *result*. It's important to understand that from a 5D consciousness perspective, however positive the intention is, if the result is born from fear, shame, or blame, it lacks integrity. And if anything lacks integrity or bears any of the hallmarks of 3D, it cannot find a place in 5D.

No matter which side of the fence we stand, we can still come into Oneness when we are whole and healed.

Yet, so long as we cling to our egos, believing there is a right way to do something and those who differ are wrong or immoral, we remain trapped in a self-destructive loop.

The appeal behind modern cancel culture is how easy it is to justify it in the name of helping the underserved or oppressed. However, the issue with it is the ease with which it can happen, how a person or persons filled with unhealed Shit and anger and armed with a few simple words can target a particular person, institution, or practice and destroy their reputation, relationships, and livelihoods.

We've seen this level of destruction of personhood—if not worse—before, yet because we are here to usher in 5D, the destruction feels even more personal, the attacks more far-reaching. Cancel culture armies are far too emotionally detached to understand that their level of destruction pits them against the light, as opposed to being champions of it. This kind of ignorance will have two results: the first keeps them stuck in 3D and their Shit unhealed, and the second widens the chasm of 3D and 5D, which becomes more challenging to straddle.

Now, more than any other time, the struggle has become the appeal. Victimhood earns us more points, and virtue-signaling victimization under the guise of inclusivity, positivity, and self-acceptance doubles those points. We've turned canceling into an art form, ready to strike the instant an idea is expressed that runs counter to our ideal. But that ideal ceases to be the ideal of Oneness once we become victims. Rather, it becomes the salve to ease the pain of whatever we decide caused our pain. And when we hold up our pain and use it as our guiding light, it only guides us to more pain because that is what pain and victimhood do. They drive us further into that hole until they occupy the driver's seat.

Cancel culture has a firm grip on our society and interactions because we haven't yet grasped that Oneness isn't a right-or-wrong concept. Moreover, opposition at this stage of the 3D-to-5D transition isn't a bad thing. On the contrary, it's necessary because it forces us to contend with every single idea, notion, principle, and thought that perpetuates Separation or enables our disempowerment. And we need to contend with them to:

1. Bring us through our healing to reach a place of peace;
2. Allow our personal peace to build the foundation for 5D consciousness; and
3. Develop the discernment required to live a life of integrity whereby all we are, say, and do is an extension of our divinity.

Noble attempts to cancel a person's viewpoint ignore the reason they hold that view. Refusing to even acknowledge those reasons, whether or not we agree with them, keeps us at an impasse. The way through is to accept that we all have reasons for upholding our values and beliefs.

When we come into 5D, we will do so as divine beings, which means none of us will carry the Shit that divides us because we'll see that nothing really divides us apart from what is on the surface. But we have to focus on the larger picture and see ourselves within that larger 5D fabric and Oneness framework. We are one of many in this moment of change, and it serves us to remember who we are, not who we wish ourselves to be, no matter how ideal or perfect we think that person could become.

Body Language
Rhea

As we discuss on our podcast, we have four main bodies:

1. Mental: how we navigate the world through our most expanded mind, which allows us to unlock our gifts and potential;
2. Physical: how we experience our world in the most tangible way possible and the most obvious divine expression we have;
3. Emotional: how we move through our feelings in response to outer stimuli, which is the fullest expression of our divine selves (the gateway to the spiritual body), and;
4. Spiritual: the very root of our being which connects us to all that we are and moves us towards the Divine.

When it comes to our physical body, we are sold that perfection is attainable, and all it takes is control. We are assaulted by images of people whose only job is to look a certain way (and even then, those images have been doctored), so we lose touch with what a person actually looks like. As a society, we have disassociated ourselves from our bodies; they are no longer part of us, they belong to us. We have turned our bodies into commodities that need to be manipulated to suit the image we think we need to present—which is dangerous at best and suicidal at worst.

In *Blaze of Glory,* I explained that karma uses every single one of our relationships to wake us up. My relationship with my body was no different. I had become so used to blaming it for every inch of my unlovable story that I had unwittingly tricked myself into believing that the enemy was the inches I was unable to shift. That meant I carried the remnants of my karmic hangover on my thighs and my ass, whilst wondering if my life could ever really change when my appearance hadn't.

Except it wasn't my appearance that was the issue. It was the perception of my appearance and what I believed that precluded me from experiencing. I had created a shield so that I could be invulnerable to the pain of being alive whilst lamenting that no one could ever see me. I had created an excuse for why things had never worked out in my favor whilst wishing they would. And I had created my suffering just to prove that I was suffering, whilst bitching that I didn't want to suffer anymore.

Separation is a bitch. It takes our inherent knowing that we are perfect as we are and twists it so that we believe we always have something we need to fix. It keeps us as constant works in progress where we are always trying to achieve a better image whilst preserving the one we already have. But when we focus on self-improvement to the degree that it becomes self-immolation, we leave ourselves with nothing to fix because we have rendered ourselves into nothing, too.

That is how powerful we are. As much as we can bitch about it, in its own way, it really illustrates the point. We can literally render ourselves meaningless by ignoring our own perfection and trying to emulate someone else's ideas of what perfection should be. We take all of our power and we use it against ourselves and fear that power at the same time, leaving us in a catch-22 that we don't know how to get out of.

Liz has explained that when we are stuck in a catch-22, it is usually karma at work. It's in the dilemmas that tell us we are screwed if we do, and we are just as screwed if we don't. So, often we try to settle for something in the middle, afraid to take one step in any direction in case that's the one that lands us on our ass. We don't often realize that those are the very steps we need to take. It doesn't matter which way we move, as long as we move somewhere.

My preoccupation with my looks became an addiction and an excuse, especially as I could never hide my body as much as I wanted to. My ego had created a reason for my suffering, and as such, I treated my body like the enemy: punishing it with diets when I had the energy and punishing it with food when I didn't. I could never be perfect until it was perfect, too, but I couldn't fix it no matter what I tried.

I also couldn't see it properly either. So strong was my disconnect from my physical body that I didn't realize that by hating it, I was hating myself. My body wasn't part of me; it just stood in the way of what I desired. I was creating the problem, perpetuating it, and then blaming myself for it whilst believing that I was the victim. I didn't work on accepting myself and my power. I was too busy focusing on getting everyone else to accept me in my powerlessness.

I hid all my light under the cloak of expectations—expectations that were never true. I wasn't fulfilling my purpose, and as a result, I was wearing my pain. Until I realized that my body wasn't stopping me from doing anything (it was my disconnect from it), I would be stuck in the cycle of hating my physical body.

My issue had nothing to do with the size of my thighs, the length of my hair, or even the color of my nails. It had everything to do with the distorted self-perception that I believed I was stuck with. My body wasn't a vehicle for my desires, it was how I experienced them. Until I could see that, I would be splitting myself into attractive parts and parts I wanted to hide—especially if I kept telling myself that how I looked to others was more important than how I felt.

When we feel happy, bright, and proud of ourselves, that is the experience that we bring into the world. Whereas, when we are feeling insecure, no matter what anyone else tells us, our perceptions will not change. We may tell ourselves that what someone else thinks of us is the most important factor (especially when it comes to our looks), but what we look like is just as subjective as how we feel. We don't spend our lives in someone else's head, we spend them living, having experiences, and allowing our bodies to carry us through the world. So, in more ways than we want to admit, how we look means far less than anything else about us.

Moreover, to fully experience our lives, we need to be in harmony with our minds, hearts, bodies, and spirits. We cannot be present when we are wondering about the size of our thighs, the frizz in our hair, or the hole in our jumper. We also can't allow ourselves to physically connect to another without being in our bodies first (especially as in *A Karmic Affair*, we explained how sex helps us shift the perspectives of ourselves and others). But when we allow our insecurities around our physical bodies to dictate how and when we show up, we miss the opportunities to see how great life can really be.

That's the thing I conveniently forgot every time I blamed my body for my experience of the world. It wasn't my body that was the issue, it was my unwillingness to see what my body could do and how it would be received. I wouldn't be able to believe that someone else would find me attractive unless I saw the attractiveness myself, and I wouldn't be able to appreciate all the joy that my body could facilitate unless I could appreciate that it was what allowed me to be alive.

All Of Me

By allowing myself to remain in a karmic standoff with my body, even when I no longer had karma holding me back, I stuck myself in a limbo that lasted far longer than necessary. I also didn't allow myself to understand that it wasn't about my body at all. Rather, it was my view of my physical world that I was projecting onto my physical body.

Coming to terms with my physical body and appreciating it for what it was rather than what I thought it needed to be, was a big deal for me. I'd never imagined that I would free myself from the cycle of punishment and relief that came with being in my body, let alone appreciate and enjoy it. But the more I saw what my body facilitated, the more I also understood the karmic undoing process in a different light.

I thought creating a new life meant destroying the old one, which was an idea that made me uncomfortable. I thought it required losing everything I loved along with it. It was a constant tug of war with myself—trying to do things differently without wanting to do very much at all. But that meant I wasn't just a creature of habit, I was a creature of stasis and not a happy one. It didn't seem possible to lay down my defenses, but in keeping myself the same, I prevented myself from experiencing better, and my world remained a reflection of who I was rather than who I had become.

I believed that to change my life, I had to become the opposite of everything that I'd been before—someone with no fixed abode who wandered aimlessly across the globe with only the Om and a passport (ideally wearing a crop top). But as much as I wasn't the epic wanderer, I also wasn't the person who could be content with staying in the same place anymore. That meant even though I wasn't going to strap on my hiking sandals any time soon, something had to give.

To have a karma-free life, we have to live it. It doesn't serve us to keep going back and picking up the pieces we've lost or looking for a silver lining amid the destruction that follows us around. We will remain stationary until we destroy ourselves. But it's not about figuring out what we want and going for it, only to turn back at the first hurdle because the world isn't set up for people making their own choices and it working out in their favor. It's about taking risks, seeing how they pan out and eventually understanding that they were never risks at all. It's also about understanding that the things that matter to us matter for a reason. Unless we have the courage to find out why they do, we won't find out who we can be without the weight of our old worlds holding us back.

I had been settling for a life that I wasn't sure was real because I was refusing to make it real. I hesitated at every step because I wanted to be swept off my feet whilst worrying that I could be swept away. That meant I didn't create anything new, and all the power that I'd uncovered lay dormant. But the only way that I would change the way I saw my physical body would be to see that body in action. That's when I could understand how powerful it really was.

Our physical body is the gateway to our physical world. Sure, I could imagine a different life from my couch, but I would never believe it was real until I had lived it. We can't build a new world through only our emotions, our minds, or even our connection to something larger. We also build it by moving, touching, dancing, kissing, holding hands, and bringing it to life. I couldn't do new things unless I was going to take the steps and actually be in new places.

That's why consciousness is so important. My physical body wasn't the full definition of my being, just as much as my emotional or mental state wasn't, either. It was a part of me that needed to be reunited with Love—just like everything else.

That was the key to breaking the self-flagellating narrative that was driving me to insanity: Love. When I followed my heart and broke my own rules, I also broke out of the limitations I had placed upon my physical body. I saw that I was capable of achieving everything I desired, and what I looked like when doing so had no bearing on the result. And the more I shone my light, the more I saw that light within myself—not just in my choices but also in my presence. I saw the beauty that I had once dulled, and I took pride in what I looked like rather than hiding it away.

We don't need to take a wrecking ball to our lives so that we can have a fresh start. Not only is that fairly counterintuitive, but it also keeps us in a cycle that we can no longer sustain. We end up reinforcing the notion that there is a finite amount of joy available, and we have to suffer to be rewarded. So, rather than create a meaningful change, we merely layer on the semblance of change and convince ourselves that everything will be better.

This doesn't mean we must lose what we value to discover something better. Despite what we have been taught to believe, there is no limit to fun, Love, or the possibility for more. The only thing we stand to lose when we don't go after everything we desire with all of our hearts is the belief that we can't have it all and more.

My body dysmorphia caused dysmorphia with everyone else, too. I didn't see them for who they were. However, when I embraced that my human experience was mine to make it what I wanted, I embraced the body that facilitated it (which meant listening to myself without judgment or shame and knowing that it was enough) and was able to connect to others differently and have the experiences I always thought were never meant for me.

I didn't need a fresh start, I needed to see that the only thing standing in the way of everything that I desired—and more—was the belief that I couldn't make it happen for me. It wasn't about walking away from everything because I wanted to keep moving forward. Doing so would only keep me in the same pattern of ignoring my desires whilst expecting a new reality to miraculously appear.

And if my karmic adventure had taught me anything, it was that all those yummy experiences would only show up when I was an active participant in my life.

Whether it was taking a flight and being uncertain of what awaited me on the other side, taking on a new project, or giving room for a relationship to evolve past what I was familiar with, I saw what my life could really look like free from all my karmic binds. My relationships deepened, my experiences widened, and I gained the confidence to keep going until changes for the better became my new normal. I could be the best version of myself—shining my light and having a great fucking time doing it. That was my own beauty, and in embracing it, it blossomed.

Life after karma never begins with the biggest unimaginable jump. It starts with a series of steps that become bigger the more powerful we become. Thing is, it's okay to take things slowly. In fact, it cannot be a switch that gets turned on overnight. All we have to do is enjoy who we are, even for a moment, to create more and more of those moments if we feel so inclined. Eventually, those moments become the norm rather than the exception. We can be in different situations and enjoy ourselves in different ways—regardless of what we look like doing it.

Against All Odds
Liz

We allow our mental bodies to rule our lives in 3D because they give us the necessary means and support to survive Separation. We need those abilities to anticipate fallouts and establish a course of action. We could logic our way through polarity, reason out right from wrong and good from bad, weigh the consequences of our choices, and allow our egos to spare us from any unnecessary grievance. Yet, in using our mental bodies to spare us undue suffering from our karma (which there's no escaping anyway) and relying upon them for tasks and relationships, we have burned them out. By burning them out, we have hampered our capacity to reach full consciousness and higher consciousness.

The problem with this is that we've slowed down our evolution. Spiritual evolution, which supports humanity's evolution, requires us to come into full consciousness, and it isn't possible when our mental bodies are running on fumes.

"You can do anything you set your mind to" (thanks for this, Ben Franklin) is often taken to mean that accomplishment in life rests solely upon the mind (the pressure). While it's true that it certainly helps to have clear goals, life in 3D has tormented our mental bodies, put them through the wringer, and compromised their integrity. As a result, if one of our bodies is weakened, the others (physical, emotional, and spiritual) suffer as well because their development is forced to slow down to catch up—which hinders our evolution in 3D.

So long as there is a body that's more prominent than the others, we won't move forward because they're not meant to operate individually or irrespective of one another. If they did, we'd compensate by overcorrecting with another body, which would throw our bodies and, consequently, our consciousness out of whack. Our bodies need to function harmoniously, always in line with one another, to serve our highest good and help us realize our fate. That's always been the point of karma: to bring our bodies back together in wholeness so we can live our lives in a place of peace.

Peace moves us out of karma and onto the early steps of our fate. It provides the compass for the initial phase of our lives when we are no longer locked within the bounds of our karma, which dictates how we live. But the initial choice to pursue our path may feel more like entering WWIII than a walk on the beach, because to get to where we need to go, our lives require a bit of blowing up before we can see our paths clearly. Rather than bring us peace, it may fill us with trepidation and present nerve-racking moments that make us question our life's purpose, leading us to wonder, "Was it always supposed to be this hard?"

The answer is *yes*. Always. Ending Separation is no small feat. It can't happen with the snap of our fingers or by merely willing it away. It requires painstaking work on our end to sift through what feels like endless amounts of trauma and stories that bring us to heel every lifetime. We are all here for our growth and evolution, and we aren't going to leave until we avail ourselves of every lesson and opportunity for growth that life on Earth makes possible.

We've come here to help usher in 5D Oneness consciousness by making space for the end of 3D Separation consciousness, so we have been on the ride of our lives. But we're never going to get off this ride until we reach 5D, having divested ourselves of everything: our karma, our fears, as well as our egos, while also having wired in enough compassion, peace, and hope.

While all previous lifetimes were about evolving through our karma and gaining wisdom through our experiences, this lifetime is entirely about transcending all the things that define our lives and, by extension, our world. We can only do this because it's time for 3D to show itself the door. The timeline is finished—kaput. Once it's done, we can't possibly conjure it if we tried because our consciousness has shifted to such a degree that we can no longer exist in Separation. It wouldn't feel normal to us. We could certainly try. Yet, the more whole we feel internally, the less comfortable we would feel splitting ourselves to hold Separation again.

Something Happened On The Way To Heaven

Outside of free will exists something more powerful: divine will. It's the full power of the Divine that is absent of, and free from, fear. This power can only exist when we no longer have our core fear guiding us—or misguiding us, if you will. While free will pushes against the boundaries of our fears and perceptions that may be limited by what bit of ego we have left, divine will has no limitations or obstacles to work around. When we are aligned with our most divine selves, nothing stands in our way anymore.

When we are utterly and firmly attuned towards the Divine, we are fully in step with our own divine presence on this earth plane, so not only are we entirely rooted in our divinity, but we are walking on that divine path in all we say, do, think, and experience. To do this as quickly and as painlessly as possible requires the following five things:

1. Understand that no matter what we think we know, we don't really know.

We think we know better when we have polarity informing our rules. However, life in 5D, especially in these early years of foundation-building, appears like a chaotic, disordered free-for-all. We move out of our limited karmic existence and into the larger fabric of our fate, so we won't know our left from our right or good from bad. Instead, we'll face innumerable opportunities and possibilities, and it will be challenging to discern which way to go and how to get there. So we'll figure it out as we go along, pivoting and turning to keep up with the pace of our unfolding consciousness.

The key will be to hold fast to ourselves. Again, this is why karma is so critical, as is ego-shedding, because we're much more apt to develop according to our personal growth and evolution as opposed to attaching ourselves to anything or anyone else.

2. Accept that life will be much more different than we believed it would be in 5D Oneness.

There will be no flying cars, nor will there be a single world order (at least, not for several generations). 5D, while utopian in concept, will seem less so in practice because while our souls may be enacting this divine blueprint for Oneness consciousness, humankind has to be on board.

Switching consciousness isn't easy. There are myriad ways for us to exist. We all may shit, fuck, sleep, and work, but we all do it differently, at different times, in different places, in different languages, while looking quite different. While we may not be different at our core, we have to learn how to contend with our surface differences before we understand our Oneness.

There is so much more to our growth and evolution that we will diverge more and more if we cannot transcend those superficial divisions that define us. But humankind regards difference as the enemy (because it is), so the only way to move out of that is to see that there is absolutely nothing about our differences that inherently threaten one another. This will take a generational shift because too many still hold the world and others in Otherness (which is holding others in the state of being the Other, as opposed to just different). Until we can eliminate Otherness, Oneness will remain out of arm's reach—which it certainly can if we continually give ourselves over to Otherness, petty bullshit, or our karmic suffering.

3. Try and try again.

5D is not inherently natural to us. We've had too many lifetimes in Separation to assume that Oneness will come easily. Moreover, we've never really pursued our purposes or missions so ardently because never before has our evolution depended so heavily upon them.

So we will get it wrong, depending on how attached we are to outcomes, and we may have to get creative with our lives to adapt. While there is no such thing as right and wrong in 5D, we'll know when something isn't going to serve us; and that's when we have to figure out how to try again.

This is critical to our success in 5D. We cannot live out our purposes or missions if we do not give ourselves space to experiment, space to expand beyond our perceived limitations, or space to imagine myriad possibilities that exist on the other side of this life. It's time to have fun with this idea rather than being scared to death of it.

In 5D, success will have little to do with monetary or ego fulfillment but with the evolution that our myriad experiences allow for. So, when we can look at something we most desire and pursue it, we can feel success is possible.

4. Stop expecting the world to conform to old ideology.

When we are no longer in the throes of 3D, anything seen as the solution to the injustices or inequities of Separation will become baseless. This will take time for people to grasp because fear makes people want to cling to the old; even if it didn't work then, we want it to work now. But it won't because it can't. So rather than attempt to drag old concepts and ideologies from 3D into 5D, it would serve us better to release ourselves from the binds of Separation completely and utterly.

When we do, we can finally be free to create a wholly new life in an entirely new world where the faces are familiar, and the streets look the same but are filled with a new energy that flows with compassion, humility, and tolerance. Just because we don't have all the answers doesn't mean we won't figure it out. But we'll get there a lot faster if leaders and influencers cease shoving these imperfect ideas down the throats of those who deserve 5D perfection.

Divine perfection is understanding and acknowledging that everything and everyone is an extension of the Divine, and as such, however they are and whatever they do is just as perfect. When we acknowledge this perfection, we no longer have to hold anyone to an ideal that was merely an ego projection in 3D.

5. See everyone for who they are, not who we need them to be.

The more we move away from our karmic stories by healing them and burning out our fears, as well as bidding *adios* to our egos, the closer we come to holding the powerful and divine image of ourselves. There isn't anything this powerful and divine person can't do that isn't in line with their fate. So our need for others to fill the void that Separation creates leaves when that emptiness is healed and we connect to that divine person.

What's critical to understand is that the longer we stay out of our power by not taking full responsibility for our lives in every area, the more challenging it becomes for others to relinquish their power over our lives. That kind of power increases the more we feed it with our own powerlessness.

Almost everyone who is in body at this point in time is here for Oneness consciousness (as I mention, some are here to uphold Separation). But everyone, no matter where they are from, who they are, or what they have done, is capable of 5D. The only criterion for anyone to come into 5D is a strong desire for more than what they are currently experiencing.

Every soul is here for more. That's the point of incarnation in this lifetime: to get the most out of our human existence and move the whole of humankind out of Separation and into Oneness. The only way to do that is to come into body and rediscover, as quickly as humanly possible, our divinity, which is often forgotten when we enter Separation.

The move to 5D takes time because life on Earth is a dense experience. Our souls can expand in a matter of moments when we have divine experiences, but when in body, burdened by the literal and figurative weight of our bodies and memories, it takes longer than a minute to work through all of it.

While that's a scary prospect, it's an exciting one because it means we can leave behind all the bullshit that came with life in Separation, all the Otherness, ego posturing, and judgment that tears us asunder over and over again, lifetime after lifetime. In the place of all that Separation, we experience a life of freedom, which can only happen when we follow our hearts and express our perfection as we live out our purpose.

Hand In My Pocket
Rhea

We all have the same core fear that we are not *good enough*—that if we lose control, we will be found out—and to mitigate that, we must appear perfect to others before ourselves. The very essence of our fear is that we cannot be ourselves because then we will not lead the lives we desire. As a result, our egos assimilate the written and unwritten rules of our society (be it through the media, socialization, or perception) and figure out the exact parameters in which we can operate.

If we cannot achieve our expected notions of perfection for whatever reason, we tend to lower our standards, settle even further, or blame ourselves and try to change to succeed in whatever endeavor we put our minds to. Often, however, what we miss is that it's not our problem. It's a symptom of a far larger problem that lies in Separation and is perpetuated by our belief structure that has attempted to assimilate it whilst remaining whole.

This is an impossible endeavor. We cannot be ourselves whilst trying to change ourselves. We cannot be fearless whilst still being scared that we could fuck it all up by exposing too much. And we cannot be whole when we are trying to cut ourselves up into pieces. If the stories that we tell ourselves about who we are inform our perceptions of the outside world and how that relates to us, that, in turn, informs our choices. We interact with the world defensively, and we channel our power into running away from our fears rather than actualizing our desires.

No matter how many affirmations we recite to compel ourselves to believe the opposite, we cannot do so unless it comes from a full-bodied place. As Liz says in *A Karmic Introduction,* "Life sucks until you die, or life might suck until you figure out why" (one of the coolest phrases she's come up with, in my opinion). Whilst she explains that the *why* is karma, I had the fantastic job of explaining the *how*.

When we are in our karma, we tend to rely heavily on our minds, which is a small part of our mental body and is where our fears and egos reside. We calculate, assess, and keep ourselves safe from the potential hazards that come with being alive. But when we operate from the core fear that we are not *good enough*, we reinforce the belief that we are avoiding. That fear informs our behavior, and we end up creating self-fulfilling prophecies—we look for ways to protect ourselves from our fears, but in doing so, we rob ourselves of the chance to find out if they are true.

Thing is, being human in Separation sucks. We don't allow ourselves to be who we really are and choose what we really want whilst telling ourselves that this is the only way to survive. The last thing anyone wants is to open a cupboard and find a bunch of skeletons in it. Worse yet, if they've convinced themselves the bodies had long disappeared.

So we buy the magic potions when they offer us everything we want with no downside. We listen to the gurus, shamans, and fortune-tellers, hoping they will show up where we haven't bothered to show up for ourselves. Even when they speak the truth, we can't hear it because unless we are asking ourselves what we want and then facilitating and experiencing it as a result, nothing will make us believe in our power.

I relied on spirituality to save me, but it didn't work. Whether it was a psychic, a friend with "special powers," or the horoscopes at the back of a magazine, every time I had outsourced my life to some "greater" entity, things went quite wrong (I don't need to remind anyone about that fantastic November incident I mentioned in *A Karmic Affair* aptly named *November Rain*). But it wasn't just Liz. I created toxic situations with Guidance, influencers influenced my actions to my detriment, and every astrologer gave me another reason to freak out over a retrograde or eclipse.

That's because when we say that we "want" to believe, what we're really saying is, "Ok, fine, prove it. Show me the money, show me the magic, and show me how powerful I really am. Give me a reason so I *know*, so I can *hope*, and so I can have *faith* and *trust*." But no one can make us believe anything, no matter how badly we tell ourselves we want to believe. And no one can make us do anything that we don't want to do or make us see that we are the only ones stopping us from fully stepping into our power, simply because we don't believe that it is ours.

I couldn't see that starting a podcast with the random lady in the gym would lead me to heal all my Shitty beliefs. But it did. I couldn't see that sharing my experiences would help others do the same. But it did. I couldn't see that taking every step at every moment was creating the life I wanted. But it did. Even when I didn't know why or how it would work out, it always did. That wasn't because I was super smart or great at feeling things, it was because there was more at play. It was because I was designing it as I went along.

I knew how to change my life. If all those years of Liz's support and Guidance's pushy advice taught me anything, it was that if I didn't know what to do, all I needed to do was take a step towards what brought me happiness. I had the power to decide everything in my world, from why I was here to what I was going to do about it. And I always did. That's why, when I found my light and maintained it throughout my daily existence, I understood Oneness in action.

From this place, I saw my life could be *better enough*. My life showed me greater possibilities, and I wanted to explore them fully, not just be aware that they existed. I knew I was capable and responsible enough to handle it, and the more I did, the more I developed the courage to keep going. I also developed the wisdom and self-belief that if my heart was calling me to do something, it would always move me towards what I wanted, even if I couldn't see it.

As I moved beyond my karmic undoing process and saw the potential for the life I had always wanted but never thought was really possible, I realized that all that wellness makes us sick—leaving us to believe that we will always be a work in progress. That is why I have banged on exhaustively about how following my heart allowed me to realize my potential rather than just waiting for it to sneak up behind me. I listened to myself, followed my own path instead of the one others thought I should, and I realized it was all perfect for me. And as I did so, I wired in a new way of being, which reflected my full consciousness.

A Million Love Songs

I'm so bored of the phrase "growth and evolution." In fact, Liz and I have often joked that we could use it as a drinking game… but the only problem is we would be wasted before we got to the end of our first book—which is essentially the problem. If we don't allow spirituality to advance past where it has already been, we don't allow ourselves to do the same, and we will pass out before the finish line.

Growing up isn't just about shedding our identities to get bigger, it's also about burning out our old beliefs so that we allow our understanding of our world to grow with us. If we don't, we'll be wasted (not in a fun way).

I wouldn't have helped anyone in a meaningful way in my karma. I hate to say that, but as much as I don't want to admit it, everything that I would have taught would have been through the filter of my pain, where I wanted to find the answers whilst fearing what those answers meant. It wouldn't have worked, no one would have been helped, and we would have been bound by what I thought I knew rather than what I later came to understand.

I would have also missed the entire point of the exercise—allowing my karma, ego, and fears to define my work whilst substituting new rules in place of the old. I wouldn't have seen everyone's differences as another aspect of our divinity; I would have tried to make everyone all the same. I would have totally refracted the light of spirituality by looking at it through the lens of Separation rather than seeing it for what it is, and I would have made it another game to play so I could prove that I was *good enough*. My gaze wouldn't have been wide enough to see past my own myopic view of the world, no matter how expanded I thought that gaze was. I also would have assumed that to impart spiritual wisdom, I would need to act in a way that was spiritual or "woo woo" where it wasn't necessary.

When we are in Love, we are in our divinity, whereby all we say, do, and think is divine. That is spiritual enough. We aren't meant to be the same, we are just meant to recognize that, despite our differences, we have the same core. But to truly find and then experience the light of that core, we have to live.

This is why, as we grow up, we have to let our concept of spirituality grow with us. Otherwise, it will drag us back to where we were. Spirituality is one of the most incredible tools we can engage with, but we aren't meant to be here and not live. We aren't meant to be here and theorize until we lose all sense of our reality. And we definitely aren't meant to all be the same, otherwise we wouldn't learn anything at all.

Karma is simply showing us where we have given our power away and are refusing to take responsibility for it. Our fears are simply showing us where we don't believe we are *good enough* to do so. And our ego is simply showing us that we don't have to be the person we thought we needed to be happy. That's it. It doesn't have to be lofty or complicated or even include those words as long as the meaning is there.

Dark Side Of The Moon
Liz

There exists one obstacle for many, who may still encounter it even after their karmic undoing process: and that is hate. It's taken a few years and a couple of books before we could tackle this topic, namely because we needed to have enough Oneness wired in to see it for what it is and not be thrown by what's coming.

Separation and all its forces feed off hate. There was a time when this wasn't the case. When Otherness was merely an act of free will to test the extent of our personal and collective power, what underpinned our very motivation was curiosity and an immense drive to test its perceived limits. The thing about limitations is that they really don't exist in the spiritual realm. So long as we can create and destroy, we can keep going without end.

Yet, as polarity and judgment encroach on our free will, curiosity becomes dangerous and our power curbed. Since divine will cannot exist with limitations, it too has to be manipulated to retain some semblance of autonomy, even if that means choosing self-denial to survive.

This may sound counter-intuitive, but bear with me as I explain. We're here for the most divine experience there can be. It doesn't mean divine as heavenly with fluffy clouds, rainbows, and unicorns as Rhea may prefer. That, of course, is possible if we choose to create it. But there exists a multitude of options, which is the point. If anything really is possible, we have to allow for the fact that these possibilities also fall on the side of those areas of life some may prefer to ignore or avoid, namely violence and abject hate.

Ignoring and avoiding those aspects of our world is precisely why this phase of confrontation is happening. To get enough of the world to Oneness and full divine expression, we have to address all the underpinnings of our Separation experience, which isn't all rainbows and unicorns. Now, this isn't my attempt to Debbie Down this chapter (and burst Rhea's balloon), which is about the path to happiness. Rather, it's to illuminate that beast that stands in the way of our happiness.

In Separation, the fullest expression of our power could include violence because we make the choice to deny the Divine within (*I and God are not One*). As I explained before, the longer a soul remains in Separation, the more challenging it becomes to return to its fullest expression (*I Am Who I Am*) because it is long forgotten. So it takes time, a series of karmic fuck-ups, to return to ourselves and remember we are more than our human experiences in Separation have told us.

The steps towards wholeness are the steps towards divesting ourselves of this separation. Often, we reach the greatest experience of wholeness when our physical bodies expire since we can be fully reunited with our fullest selves. Yet, to shift consciousness to such a degree in this earth plane, we don't have the ease of leaving our physical bodies and starting over again. We have to start over while in body, having a complete karmic and Oneness evolution while living and breathing.

As we live and breathe our personal work, so too must we address what keeps our world in Separation. While violence was never the objective in the beginning, we have been trapped in an endless cycle of it because of our need for power. The karmic undoing process confronts the need for power. Rather than our individual need for it being siphoned through the tentpoles and supporting them, we take back our own and allow them to buckle.

So long as there is energy to feed the tentpoles, they're not going away. That's because hate, what gives rise to violence, stands in the way. While it can be understood that fear underscores hate, it's often due to our inability to connect to something or someone because *I cannot see myself in you*. Yet, when it comes to the soul's experience of hate, there's a deeper perspective we have to address.

The fear that underpins hate isn't a core one, as in an immediate result of that separation that causes the karma. It's the result of many lifetimes in deep separation or trauma that leads a soul to separate even further until a person is unable to see themselves in another, nor can they even connect to the idea that it's possible. So the resulting fear goes from *I cannot see myself in you* to *I am not you and therefore I do not know myself.*

For a soul to be so separate from itself that it cannot see or hold itself in enough light to even glimpse itself in another isn't a case of "Oh, they just had a traumatic childhood." Rather, it means they have lived in the dark for so long, whether over lifetimes or among spaces that have only held dark, that it's become all they know. When there are souls who only know the dark or can hold it long enough, there will be enough to continue to feed Separation to such a degree that it will not go away until there is nothing to feed off.

This is why we require scale in numbers when it comes to Oneness. So, for all those who can feed the tentpoles with their fear and hate, there are those who can distance themselves enough from them so that they can fill the world with their light. Now, this is not to say that we are entering a battle of light and dark, nor is the intention to stoke fear that the world will implode if we don't OM ourselves into enlightenment, stop eating meat, or pick up the pace of our healing. If we're all expanding our consciousness, we are doing our part. We have to acknowledge that not only has this violence always existed, but we can no longer stand in judgment of it. It is judgment that fuels hate and keeps us from seeing ourselves—and thus seeing the Divine in others (hence why compassion is such an important component in bringing about Oneness).

It's painful to do this because it runs against much of our wiring to not stand for a right and a wrong, as well as our perceived need for justice. It hurts to see others hurt and not want to hurt the perpetrators. Yet, it's this very cycle that keeps us locked in that part of our Separation world that only we can remove ourselves from. This takes not only an expanded consciousness to hold everyone in compassion, but it also requires us to be bold enough to stand in our fullest light because only in our light can we absorb the dark of others and not be moved by it.

Since 2018, we have been witnessing a rise in hate as we process all the unseen darkness that's held within many. For some, hate is largely repressed or suppressed, which means it's not been seen by them, either. Like releasing a corked bottle, this will seem explosive, given all the energy required to keep it buried. So, we will see large swathes of darkness cover us as we find ways to release it, either from our beings or as others do it for themselves. While we may be reaching the consciousness scale required for 5D, which relies on the majority of those still reaching for the light, it will also demand a discharging of the dark that has taken up space in the deepest crevices of our world in a short period—something we haven't experienced while holding ourselves in full or higher consciousness.

There may be moments when it feels as if all is lost or at least pointless if violence and hate keep surfacing. Perhaps for some, it will seem endless—except it's not. If we can come through the other end of our karmic undoing process, so too can anyone else if they choose it. That's what it comes down to: our choices. To commit to consciousness or to what we've always known.

The Other Side Of Life

The only difference between the world of Separation and where we are today is the potential that our consciousness can perceive. The fact that we can conceive of a world of peace instead of hate, a life of happiness instead of dread, and relationships guided by Love rather than obligation means that it's possible. It may not come to be exactly as we picture it, and we may not experience it on a global scale in this lifetime. However, the ability to transcend Separation and be guided by a larger consciousness is still a massive feat for any individual.

Healing our karma is the most empowering experience we can have because it allows us to see we have the power to do anything. The more we transcend and heal, the more we encourage others to do the same. This demands that we grow up. We cannot have Oneness if we are children seeking to be saved. Nor can our consciousness really expand if we hold others accountable for our pain and well-being. It's time we come into full spiritual maturity and take ownership of the fact that there is no rewriting the past and that our future is possible because of it, not in spite of it.

In Oneness, our sense of equity is also born from compassion that acknowledges all the pain and suffering that led up to the act. Instead, we've allowed ourselves to be chewed up by social justice and environmental causes, become lost in New Age spiritual practices that promise redemption, or give ourselves over to despair. But of course, nothing could possibly work because the work begins with us. It requires us to look within and figure out our Shit.

We do this by revisiting the point at which we became so unhappy, when we convinced ourselves to ignore it because there was no way to change it. In acknowledging our own impotence, we deny our ability to find the solution to our issue, which is the answer to the simple question: *when am I happiest?*

We seem to believe that happiness is fulfillment, deep satisfaction, and abundance. While yes, those are features of happiness, happiness is far more simplistic. It's the absence of ego. Without the ego, everything just *is*, without judgment or bearing any kind of significance. Our ability to accept everything as it is, regardless of what it is, breeds contentment, and that contentment sows the seeds of happiness. This does not negate that we can desire more; rather, we accept that we are on a forward moving trajectory while also being content with where we are in the process.

Happiness is the continuous sentiment from the inside out that we carry; it tells us we are exactly where we need to be at any given time, and it's always perfect. It's neither transient nor temporary. When we grasp happiness, it's the moment of perfection that takes root inside us and never leaves. It grows and grows and grows without end.

The moment happiness not only becomes our baseline but also our guiding force (as in *I cannot be anything but happy*), all we are, say, and do align with that happiness. This guiding force or ethos is how we move along the latter parts of our fate, which brings us to our most divine selves. It's when we can be the most divine selves that we can traverse the unwritten parts of our fate, whereby we create as we breathe. As we do this, we can no longer be governed by time in the way we have always understood it, even when it comes to the "clock of the heart," where time moves by all that brings us joy.

As our most divine selves or when in full divine consciousness, we embody the All which holds all of creation, including all concepts of time—not just linear time like past, present, and future, but all the ways we can experience the multitudinous expanse of time (everything all at once). This way, time becomes the most expansive it can be and contains all the possibilities to occur whenever we require it.

We are not ruled by a sense of internal or external clocks that dictate when we should do anything. Rather, we are on divine time, where everything happens in accordance with our evolution, so that what we do, how we do it, when we do it, and why we do it has nothing to do with our temporal existence but our spiritual one (a bit like having such a great time at a party that we wonder how it's suddenly five in the morning).

When we lose our sense of time in the 3D sense, we actually engage in divine time because our hearts are fully engaged in the present, and when we are in divine time, the present is all that matters. Eliminating our dependence on time and preventing it from dictating our days is a positive first step. However, like anything else with human evolution versus spiritual evolution, it's slow to take hold. The key to catching up is to reformulate our priorities so that the things that move us towards joy take precedence in our lives, the precursor for happiness.

Extricating ourselves from our human sense of linear time, let alone adapting to divine time, has not been easy. We cannot turn it off like a light switch, nor can we merely surrender our lives to God and hope for the best. We are human, after all, and very much grounded in a 3D reality that tells us we have responsibilities and relationships to maintain. We're not here to shirk those (unless necessary for our growth); rather, we're here to enhance our lives so that our responsibilities and relationships are rooted in happiness and desire as opposed to dread and obligation.

While we've had a taster, we haven't availed ourselves of what divine time will really mean for us. We are too inextricably linked to 3D to grasp how to move from linear time to divine time. We may wonder how we could possibly provide for ourselves while being fully engaged with joy. We could question how we could even discover what brings us joy without worrying when it will all end. And it's certainly reasonable to think that because the sun rises and sets, and because there are only so many hours in a day to be productive, time cannot be understood as anything other than a measure of how we spend it.

If we can grasp that there is more to our existence than just our physical experience of it, and that there are more of us present (our other three main bodies) as well as the many bodies that comprise our full divine selves, we can step into a much larger, more powerful life than we could have ever imagined.

The soul is active and dynamic. When it comes into body, it comes to play, learn, figure out shit, and evolve. It doesn't come here to be complacent and assume we can't have it all. When we live in complete accordance with our fate, we bring ourselves to happiness. It's that happiness that becomes the Love we literally cannot live without because it informs all we say, do, think, and experience.

I've Got You Under My Skin
Rhea

It's uncomfortable for me to think about how my sole focus for so long was partnership—how much I contorted myself, bent my will, and tried to prove how lovable I could be without feeling very lovable at all. For me, partnership wasn't about sharing light, it was about saving me from myself, whilst simultaneously trying not to be myself. But at the same time, if it weren't for that exact yearning for connection, I wouldn't be where I am today.

To be fair, from the time we are born, we exist in one form of relationship or another. To say there's more to life than our relationships negates the very thing that defines our existence. But when we remove ourselves from our relationships to make them work, we lose far more than just ourselves. We also lose the way in which to discover our power and see what we are capable of.

By defining relationships so narrowly, as the partnership that would solve all my problems and the goal that I needed to pin my life on, I missed the point. It wasn't about one person outside of me. It was about me. The more I focused on that external validation—whilst behaving in some spectacular self-sabotaging ways to ensure that I would never find it—the more I disappeared until there was barely a flicker of my light left (for further context, get into bed with *A Karmic Affair*).

It was far more complex than that; bring in my relationship with the universe, socialization, religion, family dynamics, teenage trauma, and a fair amount of body hair, my issues were a *fait accompli* the second I left the job and stayed with the boy (I often wonder, had I left the boy and stayed with the job if I would now be banging on about taxes instead of relationships). But it really didn't matter. I made something external my purpose, and in doing so, I trapped myself in my karma and gave it its potency.

What a monumental fuck-up. I made partnership my point whilst at the same time making it impossible to achieve. Even if I had found the most patient (and obsessive) partner, I would be wading in co-dependent Shit instead of personal Shit, which meant that neither one of us would be free in a two-for-one Shitty party. Moreover, my fear would have eliminated any possibility of a true union.

I was taking all my divinity, power, and light and throwing it at anyone who was willing to receive it. I was talented but squandering my potential. I had bought the line about how we are here to suffer and literally created my own suffering just so I could see that I had been creating it.

That was exactly what I was doing with my life—creating my misery through relationships whilst knowing that they were one of the most important things to me.

Problem was, I kept experiencing how much they could hurt, so I turned myself into a self-flagellating martyr who couldn't trust herself, no matter how much she tried. I didn't listen to my feelings. Rather, I listened to what I thought my feelings should be. I didn't allow myself to grow up because by making my problems everyone else's responsibility, I relinquished responsibility for myself and my relationships. I played games, relied on outdated perceptions of dating, and was shocked that I couldn't find someone to fit me when I wasn't even being myself.

Without a connection within myself, I hadn't been connecting the dots to ensure a happy ending. I was just ensuring an ending—which I've learnt are two very distinct things. Except I didn't want to live in disconnection, fear of an ending, or in my case, fear of a beginning, because it could also end someday. I believed I would only be satisfied when I was part of a pair, but when it didn't really work out as intended, I let it cloud my vision so that everything lost its value—which is what led me to say those immortal words: "Fuck This."

Nothing's Gonna Stop Us Now

Partnership made sense as the solution if the solution came from outside of me (where someone would save me from myself), but that was just another version of Separation. And that separation inside myself blinded me from seeing the answer. Until I could see that I could be loved for who I was, I would never be able to accept the love of another. In turn, I would always be living in the absence of a ghost.

How we feel about ourselves defines every other relationship we have, whether or not we want to admit it. The fears that tell us we are not *good enough* color our interactions to the point that it's all we see. Our stories create behaviors that ensure specific outcomes, and even if they don't, we morph our reality to fit the narrative we desperately want to run away from. In creating those stories, we limit our potential through the expectations that result—telling ourselves that we can only be *good enough* when certain specific criteria are fulfilled, which have been informed by the collective morality that governs us.

But there isn't one opportunity for happiness, a sole person to partner up with, a solitary job that works, or a select way to live our lives. Things working differently for different people is the beauty of our world, not the detriment. Whilst some people pray to a God, a sage stick, or even a planetary alignment, I pray on the altar of relationships because I believe they are the way through our karma and to our desires. My story throughout the *Karmic Series* attests to that.

In *A Karmic Attraction*, I explained how following my heart healed all the pieces of myself that I had either abandoned, rejected, or decided weren't *good enough*. But I didn't do those things in a vacuum. I did those things whilst interacting with others. They showed me what I couldn't see in isolation. It could have been a pattern that I was creating with numerous people (same story, different face), it could have been a belief that I was perpetuating (will I ever be chosen?), or it could have been a fear that I was ignoring (love sucks). It didn't matter. The more I listened to my heart, the more I learnt that I was capable of not only doing so but trusting it too—and then trusting it could all work out.

By the end of *A Karmic Affair,* I finally understood how much I had grown up. I wanted to see how much light I could shine and how far it could take me. My purpose was expressed through my being. I couldn't outsource it to anyone else, even if they had great eyes and a cute ass. Partnership wasn't going to fill the empty, empty space because only I could claim it. In fact, my life wasn't empty; it was just missing all the bits that kept me unhappy. That space was pure potential. All I had to do was take that grown-up self and see what happened when she walked into this new world.

We may think we understand the motivations behind a choice, but we may not truly see the real reason until much later. We can't always see that we're addressing our core fear (*I Am not Good Enough*), our karma (the physical, emotional, mental, and spiritual manifestation of that core fear), or our ego (the protection mechanism to avoid the core fear). Or sometimes all three. They will always be reflected in whatever we do until we see who we really are.

I viewed spirituality as a means to a specific goal rather than a tool to continually expand my perspective. But I couldn't see that I didn't need to prove that I was *good enough*. I needed to know it in every one of my bodies (aka becoming fully conscious) and see where that would take me.

We are here to be happy, even if we don't believe it. We are meant to become better versions of ourselves, living better versions of our lives. But until we see that it starts with our own baggage, we will carry it around until we break our backs. That difference isn't in who we were, what we thought, or who we used to share our beds with. It's allowing for a life where we're constantly learning new facets of what we can experience and achieve when we put our hearts into our lives.

All we need is the courage to follow our light. We are the ones to light up our purpose, our power, and where we are meant to go next. The more we follow that light, the more we neutralize the separation within until there is nothing left. We don't need to second-guess ourselves because we can own who we are and what we desire. We don't need to worry about our choices because whatever happens will always be in our highest good, even though we can't see that in the moment. And we don't need to settle for a life of *just enough* or even *better enough* because we can create everything we want and more.

Who Are You?
Liz

Not only is it challenging for a soul to exist in a state of Separation from the Divine, but the physical body needs a certain amount of density to sustain itself. Earth is a dense place for spirit, which makes it difficult to bring through its light. Density is merely that which gives us form so we can withstand all the elements of life on Earth. Spirit, on the other hand, is pure energy. For spirit (which is the animated soul) to come into body, it has to ground itself, utilizing whatever possible (such as food, sex, drugs, and alcohol). This requires a certain amount of lower consciousness, that is, not divine consciousness.

Yet, the longer we remain in lower consciousness, the more difficult it is to transcend it. That is why we have spent lifetime after lifetime working through this, so we can finally reach a period in our consciousness where we can experience longer lifespans to shed more of our density.

At this point in our consciousness, we recognize the Divine in ourselves, but also the Divine in others, and all things. Karma brings us into this consciousness because as we heal the pain that has taken hold of our mental, emotional, and physical bodies, we see beyond the trauma that influences our daily lives.

The less of our density that we have to contend with, the easier it becomes to connect with spirit and raise our consciousness (hence why so many spiritual arts and crafts focus on diet and movement, which can be helpful shortcuts). Although, frankly, we can get there without any extreme measures because of karma. The karmic path has us lightening our density with every choice we make that moves us towards ourselves and the Divine—because we won't require all the crutches we depend upon to live in Separation.

What lies beyond is a reality that becomes governed by our sense of divinity and our higher consciousness, which tells us we are more powerful than we once believed. That power ensures we are capable of reaching our fullest potential. When we reach this level of consciousness, we can be in full partnership with our higher self, that untouched and often untapped part of ourselves that is absent of karma and trauma. Although we might consider it our soul, our higher self is more conscious, more aware, and more expanded, while our souls are merely coded vessels awaiting animation.

What guides us through our karmic process is our higher self, which is effectively the director of this whole fucked-up play where we're both the protagonist and the villain. It also ensures that everything and everyone is in the right place at the right time and knows their lines down to a T. Our higher self is also like the best friend who holds our hair while we're slumped over a toilet after a rough night out, tells us that the person who didn't text us back is really the asshole while also acknowledging it's okay if we still like them, and stays up all night with us when we're reeling from a heartbreak. It's effectively the coolest, wisest version of us without the bullshit.

Won't Get Fooled Again

Facilitating a connection between ourselves and the Divine ultimately begins with connecting to our higher selves. Our higher self is that part that is most detached from our human experience. That detachment allows our higher self to keep us on our path to ensure that we do what we came to do and prevent our experiences in Separation from distracting us.

Our higher selves are part of the larger divine consciousness that keeps us connected to the spirit realm that allows us to retain our divine identity. They are in place for three reasons:

1. To ensure that our time on Earth, in body, serves its purpose, that is, to transcend the karmic experience and reach our divinity.
2. To keep us from falling into the abyss of Separation by reminding us of the Divine.
3. To spread light through our physical being.

To choose to be separate from the Divine is how we exist in Separation. Our higher self, which is our connection to the Divine, takes a back seat when we exercise our free will. So long as we are in body, we always have access to our higher self; but, like with all of our Guides, there's a non-interference clause in the contract that very clearly expresses that absolutely no one or no thing can influence our choices. We must be free to choose, even if that choice is to recognize our divinity to the point we don't want to choose anything else.

Usually, when the subject of channeling comes up, or mediumship, or whatever, we want to believe that we're communing with some incredibly advanced being or entity. While certain spiritual arts and crafts have us believe that we're channeling XYZ Angel, the god of fill-in-the-blank, or the Master Guide whomever, that's often the ego trying to make us believe that being able to do so makes us unique. The reality, however, is that it's often our higher self that we're accessing; it's just difficult to believe that we, even in our most expanded perspective, can be that wise and advanced.

In the process, we're taught to doubt or fear our higher self. But here's the thing: our higher self is infallible because it holds all the information contained within the larger fabric of our fate. It functions as our most relatable, accessible Guide. Our higher self knows all and sees all, whereas our Guides do not. They only know what suits their function in support of our overall objective, which is to help get us out of our karma and into our purpose quickly and efficiently. What makes this so incredible is that when we really allow ourselves to connect to and avail ourselves of the wisdom and experience of our higher self, we truly do become unstoppable.

As I said before, we really don't need our Guides as much as we believe. While the Angel stories are beautiful, and the images of fairies and devas go a long way, there's a greater truth: we are just as much a part of that large tapestry of being as they are because we are all sourced by the same thing. And because we are sourced by the same thing, we are at One. Absolutely nothing separates us from them, and we all ultimately serve the same function, which is to hold that Oneness consciousness inside of us all.

Granted, that knowledge and connection are tremendous and ensure that we always remain on our life path in the broadest way. Yet, it's our higher self that keeps the trains running on time, so to speak, and on track to fulfill our purpose and fate. Our higher self is solely responsible for the design of our lives and the blueprint of our fate. It chooses the karmic pathway that suits our soul's learning for its growth and evolution. It decides all the contracts we make for the relationships that get us to the goalposts along our path and does its utmost to keep us on track and focused.

Our higher self really doesn't get enough credit because we've been convinced for too long that our power and wisdom don't really come from us but rather are bestowed upon us should we prove ourselves worthy and deserving.

The thing is that we are already worthy and deserving. We are completely powerful enough to create the lives we wish for; we've merely forgotten how to and allowed ourselves to become hindered by all of our perceived obstacles. It's understandable. There's been too much noise, too many things getting in our way.

Our ability to connect to our higher self comes when we avail ourselves of the choice to maintain that relationship with it, which can happen at any time or juncture in our lives (often when we're feeling desperate and alone). Thus begins our awareness of the connection to the Divine and Guidance. The connection is always there; it's merely muted because of us.

Our higher selves are far more powerful and influential in our lives than most realize. We tend to credit the Guides with helping us keep our Shit together and accepting our prayers, but the reality is that our higher selves are most responsible for us living our best lives (when we've been able to), keeping us out of mortal danger, and making sure our fuck-ups aren't total fuck-ups. In short, they keep us humming along in our lives, helping us stick to our original plan to grow and evolve as best as we can under Separation circumstances.

So, between our Guides and our higher self, we are part of a larger contingent that holds our being together in both the physical and spirit realm. They allow us to remain connected and have a foothold in both realms to optimize our reality and transcend Earth's consciousness, to bring the Divine into our everyday lives. This means we have to go back to the beginning, our beginning, to ensure that we are traversing our own story and not someone else's. It also means connecting to our higher self, who is the one who will, without a shred of a doubt, get us to precisely where we need to go if we feel lost.

Love & Hate
Rhea

Our lives are created by our choices, which are based on our perspectives and how powerful we recognize ourselves to be. The point of karma is to understand that we are so powerful that we have made ourselves believe we are powerless. It uses every relationship we have to show us how we are the architects of our own demise—including the one with our higher self.

I wasn't quite sure what a higher self was, but if I had one, they were most likely the reason why things hurt so much. It was like a parent exercising tough love—I believed that my higher self called the shots, made choices, and ensured that I hit certain points in my evolution, whatever it took. It was their fault that it was a struggle to learn whatever lessons needed to be learnt. And even though it would eventually be for my highest good, it didn't feel good in the meantime.

As a result, I massively resented my higher self because I was locked in the story that someone was doing something to me rather than taking responsibility for my life. I wanted to blame someone else for my demise, but I also wanted someone else to provide my salvation. It was far easier to circle my victimhood than to accept that I was party to it (and not in a fun way). That meant my relationship with my higher self was fraught. I couldn't trust the feeling, I second-guessed the intention, and I feared the outcome.

It may have been a stretch in *A Karmic Introduction*, but by the time I understood Love in *A Karmic Affair*, it was natural. I could make conscious choices because I was using my mental, emotional, and physical bodies to inform my choices. I knew something was the right move for me if I felt excitement in my emotional body, relaxed in my physical body, or clear in my mental body. I also knew if something didn't feel right, I had to either course-correct or look for a different approach. Those choices may have been uncomfortable or even scary, but I felt they were the only choices I could make—because I was always choosing to listen to myself and follow through.

Even though my choices hadn't necessarily turned out the way I expected, they laid the foundation for something even better. I may not have known what would happen every time I followed my heart, but every time I did, I landed somewhere even greater. I also learnt something new and healed something old. The more I did so, the more I could Trust myself and allow that path I was following to unfold.

When I was in my karma, I didn't recognize that my heart couldn't think and my mind couldn't feel. But my issue post-karma was that neither could see two steps ahead, so I couldn't foresee what my choices were leading to. That meant that even though I was out of my karma, ego, and fear, I still played in the patterns that had been created in order for me to survive it. I couldn't believe that it was possible to create anything different from what I had already experienced.

Once we become conscious, we don't wait for anything to miraculously show up. Things show up as we make choices. My issue was that I couldn't understand *how* my choices were working out for me, so I couldn't trust them, although I knew that I could trust myself. This was why I couldn't trust my higher self, either. But without dealing with it, I would still be reacting from that lack of trust for infinity or, in my case, in this lifetime.

The Voice Within

I've explained how the four pillars of Trust form the foundation of Love. What I haven't explained is that these four pillars underpin the relationship we have with our higher selves and how they allow us to avail ourselves of our power. It's not our feelings alone that get us out of our karma (although that's what I initially thought when I started following my heart), it's what we access when we tap into those feelings—a deeper power that brings us peace when we exercise it. The issue is, to have that kind of power, we can't use our emotions, mind, or body (alone or together). We have to recognize that we are also divine and have the power of the Divine in our arsenal.

Our spiritual body is our connection to the Divine. It's the part of us that sees there is more to us and our lives than just our current physical reality. It's also the part of us that knows how to create a life in joy that expresses our purpose. When we listen to it, we follow our unique path and become a more expanded version of ourselves.

For many, becoming conscious is enough. To heal our Shit, to navigate the world from that space—creating opportunities for better rather than worse—and to live knowing that we can choose how to act and react in every moment of our lives is a feat few have experienced. Except there is more. That is why the karmic undoing process is so invaluable. It also lays out the steps for what comes next. Not because I say so, or because Liz waves her pendulum and Guidance agrees, but because once we are finished, we can take responsibility for who we are and what we desire.

That can be a stretch for many of us to reach, but it doesn't have to be. Nor does it have to be lofty or super spiritual, either. To change our world, we have to embrace how powerful we really are and commit to it unwaveringly. In doing so, we use our power to create the lives we desire with our light (aka our Love) rather than live in the absence of it. The very act of accessing that power means we show up as ourselves in every facet of our lives. So, as we take the light we have connected to within and express it outwardly, we allow for other opportunities and outcomes that would otherwise elude us—simply because we aren't limiting our possibilities to what we already know (and often don't like).

I learnt that it was through my heart that I could access my spiritual body where the pillars of Trust resided—which meant my divinity was just as much a part of me as my other bodies. I simply needed to acknowledge what I had already achieved and tap into the courage I'd gleaned to keep going. That was the gift my higher self was offering—the fact that I could Trust myself—as well as the experiences I could access when I incorporated that knowing into my life.

Only I could know what my desires really were, and only I could experience them. No psychic, fortune-teller, or even best friend could know more than me about my life. I had been the one to make the choices to come out of my karma, and no one could tell me what to choose. I wouldn't have gotten where I needed to go.

That was what my higher self pushed me towards: healing myself and stepping into my power to get me to where I could break the final ties of Separation and fully express it without any constriction. My higher self helped me get rid of all of my Shit so that I could finally be free to create the life I desired.

But there's more. It wasn't just my higher self that had my back. I was that higher self because I was listening to my own heart and I was the one who was acting accordingly. I was the one who got me out of my karma, no one else—which meant I was that higher self I'd been stressing about the whole time.

The One granting all my wishes and the One facilitating them in the real world were the same person, and they were me. It felt like they were conflicting when I saw the power was outside of myself, but when I saw it wasn't, I finally accepted that I'd been the one to make every choice, that I was the one who was responsible for my life, and that my desires could be made real in my physical world.

That meant my higher self wasn't separate from me because we had the same goals. We weren't different entities. We were One, just as the rest of my bodies were too. And if working together created the miracle of a karma-free life, the possibilities were no longer limited to my narrow ego perceptions of my future.

Some would say that the universe communicates to us via a gut instinct, a knowing, a seeing, or even a little voice inside our heads. But that isn't the universe, it's our higher self. Our higher self is that light we shine, and it's the best guide we can ever have because it's us owning, knowing, and expressing just how special we really are. It's us taking a leap of faith, trusting that we can make choices for our happiness, and hoping our heart's desires will present themselves.

This means it's effectively the best guide we can ever have because it isn't just a guide (that we don't share with anyone else), but as it's our higher self, our connection to the Divine is simply another connection to ourselves. It also means that we are the most powerful beings in our world.

My higher self was a part of me, not powerful over me, but in casting myself as a victim, I made myself the perpetrator, whether or not I wanted to admit it. It wasn't about acknowledging my higher self when things went really well or horribly, it was about acknowledging that my divinity was a part of me. I wasn't just my feelings, thoughts, or movements, I was all of them at once.

The uncertainty wasn't scary, it was an opportunity. By accepting that my higher self was me, I remained in higher consciousness and ensured that my choices always aligned with my fate. I was the One thing who would always have my back, and the unknown was a playground, not a minefield. All that evidence that I was searching for outside of myself was staring me in the face. I had changed my life, and I was the One who made it all happen—simply by exercising Love.

Take Me To Church
Liz

We are at a point in our spiritual evolution where we can no longer hide who we are. That's Separation 101. To survive 3D means compartmentalizing our lives and fitting in in whatever way we can, doing whatever is expected of our gender, race, and socio-economic group, while pushing aside all the other parts of ourselves that don't fit in with the status quo. Life in 3D is measured by outward appearances. Inwardly, we can be a heaping mess of unresolved karmic Shit, but it doesn't matter as long as we appear to be managing.

There isn't anyone on this earth plane at this given moment who hasn't lived this way. We do so because entering 3D requires a shield because if we enter as fully integrated, divine beings, we won't last a day in Separation. So we learn early on what's acceptable and what isn't. We rely on social cues, family units, and well-meaning teachers to show us the way. The more determined we are to burn out our karma (like Rhea), the better students we become (gold stars for Rhea!).

Yet, the longer we receive validation and acceptance, the longer we deny those parts of ourselves we hide, namely our wisdom. Wisdom is the result of our spiritual selves becoming fully integrated into our human experience. It allows for all the knowledge we hold at our most divine core to become interwoven with the fabric of our everyday human life. Never before have we had an opportunity to live this way, since Separation demanded that we compartmentalize our lives and experiences.

To hold wisdom while living in Separation means having to live apart from others. These people aren't necessarily recluses, outcasts, or even outliers as much as they are so in touch with their heightened awareness that they can't be around others who aren't. The dissonance is too great. So they keep their social circles small and their family units tight-knit, and they are most certainly prone to coping mechanisms that numb their awareness.

This is no longer the case as new generations of wise and enlightened souls come into body and safeguard their wholeness. They are here to pave the way for even larger numbers of souls to come into body, who will be the ones to bring humankind through the first stage of total Oneness, which is due to begin around 2034. Or, they are here to help facilitate the end of 3D Separation. While 3D has reached its completion, endings on a human scale take a long time.

This slowness can be incredibly frustrating. Coupled with the ever-expanding consciousness and the resistance to Oneness (many have begun to see life in 3D for what it is, but rather than hold it in compassion, they judge it), as well as the lack of preparedness for this change—it seems as if we've been on the brink of our very own self-destruction since 2012, wondering if we're insane. Or perhaps the world is just insane, and we're just here for the ride.

The reality is that it's neither. To reach the level of awareness required to come into basic consciousness, and to facilitate the transition from 3D to 5D, means becoming aware of Separation and all the damage it has wrought. While this awareness has been emerging for some time, it hasn't emerged quickly enough to prepare enough people for the beginning of the end of 3D. Since many are slow to adapt, the transition is taking time and will likely take longer than anticipated.

The lack of patience, tolerance, and compassion is hurting everyone, especially those souls who struggle to maintain their wholeness. They want the world to match their Oneness ideal, the one they came into body to help create. But the difference between their external and internal worlds has become so great that many are losing the will to keep going, opting for violence or settling for victimhood. It's not their fault the world isn't necessarily ready for them, but they do bear the responsibility of doing better. And it begins with finding their wisdom again. This is where compassion can help.

Compassion isn't about being generous or kind or sincere or any new-age platitudes. Rather, it's about being in step with ourselves and the causes of our suffering. When we show ourselves compassion, we accept that we are where we are because of where we were, that moment in time when we didn't know any better and made a particular choice. It's not because we were wrong, but rather we just didn't have all the information.

Compassion understands that we will always know better when we act from our divine selves. Most of us are not there—yet. That is okay. It takes a lot of focused work to divest ourselves, not just of our karma but of our wiring that holds Otherness and exclusivity, that doesn't want to believe that someone could be like us for fear that makes us less special or diminishes that tenuous self-belief we've worked so hard to build. But our divinity knows better. Our higher selves are here to help get us there, and our faith—that untouchable, indelible belief in our capabilities, the reason that we get up every day despite our challenges—will continue to drive us.

Church Of The Poison Mind

Our fairy tales, folklore, and myths reflect the knowing that something exists outside of our humanness. The stories about God, the devil, gods, deities, and fairies give us context for that spirit we somehow know exists despite being unable to pinpoint its origin, nor are we sure if it has any real bearing on our existence.

Yet, we can't connect to this knowing because 3D consciousness—and the core fear we are not *good enough* we hold as a result—weakens that connection. We cannot have a direct connection to spirit in Separation, so religion became the surrogate for that relationship, which made

CHURCH OF THE POISON MIND

us completely and utterly dependent upon it for our life force.

Today, religion as a tentpole is upheld by what many would regard as the major faiths of the world (for instance, Islam, Judaism, Christianity, Catholicism, Hinduism, Buddhism, and Taoism). But since Separation has existed for eons, in the past, that particular tentpole was held up by any group that aimed to serve as a line to some God or gods, or even the devil. It doesn't quite matter *what* any group, cult, or organization worshiped, so long as its primary focus or belief system is centered around some otherworldly being whose very existence influenced our own.

The foundations of 3D have used God, religion, evil, polarity, and shame to uphold our subsequent subjugation of one another to alleviate our own fears of not being *good enough*. In Separation, there's no better way to prove we're *good enough* than to put it on display for everyone else to see. As a result, we become its subjects and servants, willing to do whatever we need for a reasonable or "good" life in the present life and the afterlife. It doesn't matter that there is no real "proof" of an afterlife; our fear makes us susceptible to believing that something has to be more powerful than us. Otherwise, life would be better than we know it to be, or if we have what's considered a good life, it's never a result of our own doing but rather luck, a favor from the gods, some karmic gift, or "God shining down on us."

It's the lie that helped to justify colonialism and continues to work today. People's perception or belief in their own powerlessness stems from the one thing most haven't dealt with: their core fear that they are not *good enough*. We cycle through it throughout our history and mythology, gods defeating demi-gods, deities wreaking havoc on humankind, and devil possessions among the superstitious. Then we turn around and propagate it through our own practices, shaming and battling others to establish some sort of personal power.

Even though some may have lost their faith in religion, some have turned towards New Age spirituality practices (which are just co-opted old practices) like numerology, astrology, mediumship, face reading, palm reading, shamanism, Tarot, crystal grids, yoga retreats, plant medicine, manifestation, and so on.

But we're still in fear. We're looking to everyone and their cousin who reads tea leaves for answers to our burning questions that speak to the deep and profound insecurities we hold. Will I be happy? Will I be rich? Will I die alone? Will I be famous? Will I be successful? It must be written somewhere in our fate, right? A fate that we can't possibly have written because who presumes that we have that kind of power? We don't, do we? Because if we believe we can write our fate, then that would make us more powerful than we are, more independent, and even prideful. Furthermore, it would mean we're responsible for everything that has happened and will happen.

The overlap between religions and New Age spirituality is not surprising. We, as humans, long for and crave a divine connection; we just don't know where to find it. Years of religious practices, abuses, wars, and power grabs have exhausted us, yet there has been little to fill the void. So we have merely transferred that divine desire to things that appear less invasive, more scientific, and less demanding of our time, and we conflate our faith in the Divine with faith in some chart that tells us that if we have Taurus moon, then we are only compatible with a Taurus sun who has their mars in Scorpio so long as it is in their first house.

No matter how well-intended many of these practices or religions may be, anything that was developed while in Separation or that served as a conduit between an individual soul and the Divine will lose its potency because it requires that a soul hold 3D consciousness—that is, Separation—for it to work. That isn't sustainable anymore.

To be fair, there are some "alternative" practices and teachings that have been channeled or sourced from beyond 3D. These will likely retain their efficacy so long as they remain uncorrupted by the Separation in which they are practiced. This is very difficult to do because it requires a great deal of integrity on the part of the modality and practitioner, and maintaining integrity in the age of Separation is near impossible. People falter, make mistakes, and fall prey to their egos. We see it in all areas of life, and New Age spirituality is no exception.

Never Can Say Goodbye
Rhea

Whether it was psychics, astrologers, or healers, I was adept at asking others why my life wasn't working out the way I'd planned. They would bang on about my career (yeah, yeah, I'm going to be special, but how do I make it work with this someone special?) and then tell me that my love life wouldn't start until my mid-30s (oh Shit!).

Even though I wasn't given any solutions, I took their words and twisted them to feel like solutions, expecting my life to fall into place. Needless to say, it didn't work—even when I dragged myself over the charred remains of unrealized potential, wondering who would give me the kiss of life and give me the redemption I had been looking for.

That's when I stepped into my first (and last) weekend retreat, and everything went sideways. Don't get me wrong. It's not as if the person hosting it was out of integrity or their message was not in line with something I could connect to. In a different headspace, I could have experienced something extraordinary. But at the time, I was looking to remember that there was more to my life than just my pain. I wanted context for my feelings, and I wanted something else to miraculously turn my life around in one "click."

However, when I looked around, I saw that I was just as lost as the rest of the people who were looking to the host of the workshop to save them from drowning. At that moment, I woke up. He wasn't going to fix them or me. And, if he couldn't, then I didn't see the point of believing any of it. All my faith was tied up in that one person and their message, so once I realized they couldn't provide me with the answers, my already tenuous faith fell.

It happens to most of us at some point in our lives, and often it happens more than once. A fall may not come out of some huge confrontation or seem significant to others in the context of our lives. It doesn't matter what it is, whether it's that we feel like we're unable to be ourselves or are reminded how far away from ourselves we have gotten. For me, it felt like Love was ripped out from under me, that something I could count on (my faith, hope, trust, or knowing) could no longer be relied on—almost as if I couldn't be sure that it was ever there. The moment that I doubted the very things that underpinned my point was also the moment that everything became pointless.

I shut down—until five years later, I decided to live again when one of my best friends booked me to see a kabbalah astrologist because she "thought it would be good for me." So I turned up, heard I was special, but also heard how I had some troubles that needed to be resolved… Well, she wasn't wrong.

A little light flickered, and my mind couldn't ignore it any longer. Maybe, just maybe, I was too hasty to shut everything off. Maybe, just maybe, there was a truth in all of this. Maybe, just maybe, my faith was the solution after all. For months, I did very little apart from sit on that information, until I got off the couch, put my embroidery down, and reopened my heart to a sliver of the possibility that it wasn't pointless.

Then I went full throttle. I smoked myself out of the house with sage, and I took the moon cycle very seriously. I discovered a way of looking at manifestation, which guaranteed results if I followed the program. I started doing inner child meditations, taking down whole forests with my journaling, and projected so far into the future that it became too far to reach. I learnt the theory (if we believe it can happen, it will), I learnt the hacks (don't settle because that's a test), and I learnt that I could manifest pretty much everything apart from the one relationship I actually wanted.

I didn't realize it, but I was doing the same thing again. I filled my life with the illusion of spirit rather than allowing it into my life. I taught myself astrology, I read every book I could get my hands on about mystics, I watched videos on the Law of Attraction, and I self-declared as "woo-woo." I was building myself up to fall again. And I still didn't see it, even when I befriended a small lady in a dance class who made me feel a little uncomfortable, although I couldn't explain why (that's Liz, by the way). But my fate was sealed when I proudly told that same lady that I was "woo-woo," and she told me that she was "very woo-woo" too.

Follow The Sun

Our memory of what caused us to separate from ourselves makes it hard to believe that we can experience life in any other way. For some, it may be a parent's reaction to us, a teenage misunderstanding, or even a betrayal that we never saw coming. The common denominator in these experiences is that we separate ourselves from our divine selves, and the innocence of our perceived perfection is lost.

That is what's so dangerous about spirituality in its current form. It builds people up so that we become divine adjacent, and when we realize we aren't infallible, it all comes crashing down. We are left to pick up the pieces that are scattered across our histories, not knowing which ones to leave behind. We buy into modalities that tell us to let go of our pain, detach from our humanity, remind ourselves that suffering is an educational tool, rewrite the moments that broke us, and then pretend everything is fine because we got a couple of things off our wish lists.

But what we are looking for, which we never have the courage to write on those lists, is healing the pain caused by the fall when we separated from ourselves in the first place—the healing that comes with the understanding that we never had to fall. When we write our lists, try to pass our tests, focus on the stars, look to external validation to prove our deservingness, or even turn to our work wife to predict our futures, we are really asking if it's safe for us to be our true selves again. We are asking someone to give us enough courage to hope for a better future, have faith that it will come, know that it's possible, and trust that it will be better than we could have ever imagined.

In *A Karmic Affair*, I shared the story of my final fall (it's *November Rain* again). It was pretty gnarly, and it nearly broke mine and Liz's relationship in the process. But what I didn't explain at that time was what it took for me to get back up. In some ways, it was obvious (it was a book about Love), but it was bigger than that, too. It was my power; learning how powerful I really was and learning how to wield it ensured I would never have to remember my fall again.

We don't keep falling and getting back up, as the stories would have us believe. Rather, we continue to relive the fall as if it were happening again and again. But instead of facing it, we lose ourselves in the search for the cure—all the while telling ourselves that the search is meaningless because we are, too. But without understanding that we've always been the meaning we've been searching for, and that the fall was the moment we negated our full divinity, we will never free ourselves. We will always look for the next trap door, next lesson, or next reminder that we have everything to lose, regardless of how much we may gain in the process.

That's why we keep losing. Not because there is anything to lose but because we've lost ourselves already. For someone like me, who self-proclaimed that I'm here for Love, the moment I lost my faith, hope, trust, and knowing, I lost my power and the foundations of Love I believed I was here to express. Without them, I rendered my life meaningless, and I took everything and everyone down with me. Every time I shut off my spiritual connection, I shut off my power. I shoved my higher self onto the sidelines and looked for someone else to give me that high. But in doing so, I removed the one thing I needed to bring me back to myself.

That's why we follow our hearts. By listening to ourselves and acting accordingly, the separation we experience dissipates until we are no longer separate. Every time we do, we reconnect to ourselves and our divinity, thus removing the barriers between us and our power. Our hearts make real our desires, until our reality reflects our consciousness and we are ready for our consciousness to expand evermore.

That's what Liz means by growing and evolving, which is the whole point of this karmic undoing process. We're meant to slough off every little thing holding us back from being the shiniest, greatest versions of ourselves, and then we're meant to take that version of ourselves on the ride of our lives.

That means it's up to us. We can learn from joy. We can experience ourselves differently and develop skills other than navel gazing or cursing the gods. That's why we keep trying, not because we are gluttons for punishment, but because somewhere, deep inside, we know we can.

Spirituality was never meant to save us. It's meant to bring us back to ourselves so we can create our lives rather than survive them. That's what is missing from all these spiritual influencers, social media spells, and affirmations that are being bandied about with little understanding of what can be achieved. We don't need to keep working on our stories, we don't need to unravel our histories, and we don't need to become someone new to experience new things. We also don't need to keep waiting. We just need to live and get used to living.

That was what I was missing, too. There is always more if we want more, and spirituality will get us to see that, regardless of why we think we're doing it. Every time I fell, I saw how separate I really was. But every time I engaged with spirituality in a way that felt true to me (aka Love), I remembered that I was stronger at One than separate and that I could create my own life.

As I healed, things shifted (because I wasn't fucking myself over), and I wanted more. It wasn't that I was insatiable, it was that through experiences I had in that newfound space, I naturally wanted to experience more. What was novel became natural, what was unreachable became possible, and what was afraid of the dark became filled with light.

That was the approach that helped me achieve more goals than I ever thought possible. And I knew it was possible because it had already taught me to trust myself, to know my heart, to hope for more, and to have faith that life would always keep expanding as I did—so I would never have to fall again to remember my power.

Are You Gonna Go My Way?
Liz

We haven't arrived at this emerging Age of True Enlightenment to remain split and separate from ourselves, others, and spirit. We're here to realize that we're a part of one another. To do that is to eliminate every part of Separation we hold.

The very belief in something or someone having our backs connects us to the idea that there is more to us and our lives than just flesh and bone. But faith has become a need to be saved by that something or someone, and that's not what faith is about. It's about remembering (or re-membering) who we are, so we remember all that we are capable of, which is our divine power. Yet, in hinging our faith on a savior, we kill its meaning and distort its purpose, which ultimately renders our faith useless.

When faith goes, the other three pillars buckle under the pressure. It is the connection our divine selves facilitate that opens us to our knowing, reminds us to trust what comes, and channels our desires from our hearts. Without faith, the pillars crumble like a house of cards, and everything becomes meaningless and results in complete nihilism.

How fucking devastating. To have no meaning, while awesome in its own fully detached what's-it-all-about-fuck-the-point kind of way, is how we derail and lose our humanity. Without our humanity, there is no point to this life and to our world. All the brightness, all the creativity, all that makes being in body and on this Earth plane so real and, frankly, beautifully messy is lost. While we don't have to take life so seriously that we need to find a point to everything and make everything mean something, the absence of meaning and faith kills the invisible thread that links us all.

When things become meaningless, our choices lose their potency. Again, they may not have to mean everything and be burdened with do-or-die consequences, yet if they mean nothing, they carry no power. Thus, all we do becomes so random that we may as well disengage with them. So again, what's the point?

That's the other thing about nihilism. It's the free-for-all everybody wants because no one wants the responsibility for what's to come—since we all have felt too powerless throughout most of our lives to do anything about it. So why the fuck care, especially if those at the top of the tentpoles are pulling so many strings and we're their dancing puppets?

But it doesn't mean we can't do something about our individual lives, which is why we are so hellbent on this karmic undoing process. And frankly, that's what our will has always been about—to make up our lives as we see fit, which we can only really do once we are conscious enough to steer our own ship.

For anything to have a point, it needs to have some force or power behind it, which is exercised by the person in question. We are the ones who give power to all we do. We are the ones who decide what our choices mean to us and the impact they can have. When we operate from our divine power, we know precisely what we are doing, even if we cannot foretell all that will come from it.

Everything has a point if we decide it does, and the weight of that point comes from the weight of the power we put behind it. When we say the world can change, it really can when we put the full weight of our power behind anything we do. If we are looking to make a meaningful change, we have the capacity to do it with our full intention.

But getting to that power is a challenge. All the years of life in Separation and exercising our free will to remain separate means that it's not our human nature to automatically recognize the Divine since we've been separated from ourselves for too long. Karma has become the channel by which we reclaim our divinity one Shitty scenario at a time.

As we come into Oneness, our capacity to exercise our power is only possible when we are supported by faith—again, not the belief in some savior but the faith that we really have our own back and can shape our lives as we wish. The idea that faith teaches us to endure or sacrifice for some later payoff isn't faith at all. It's subservience to the powers of the tentpoles; the Divine didn't come here to suffer, it came to know its power.

Every time we exercise our faith, really knowing that we do things because we can (not because we have to), we show ourselves time and again that things will work out. When we do so from the most conscious place we can, we build that faith, which expands the other three pillars so that our Oneness gets stronger. This is how we move from exercising our free will to divine will, whereby all of our choices become an expression of our divine selves.

I Wanna Dance with Somebody

Peeling back the layers of who we are only happens when we can honestly, frankly, and openly reconcile our past with our present. Once we've attuned ourselves to the Divine *and* walked the path of our fate in accordance with divine time, we can bring ourselves to the freedom we need to live our lives in Oneness.

The past is truly the past. It's only relevant if it keeps cropping up in repeating patterns. When that occurs, we're being reminded that we're missing something, either an important lesson or a piece of wisdom that was left behind because we're so inclined to move past whatever is uncomfortable.

We can only come into our wisdom once we've braided all the pieces of ourselves back together. Since everything left in that closet is a part of us and bears some significance, we cannot leave it behind. Absolutely nothing gets left behind in Oneness, not even those old parts of ourselves. They may not be who we are now, but those pieces of us always require resolution, forgiveness, and peace.

That means we need to find everything we've left behind and integrate them. However, we often cannot face some of those old pieces of ourselves until our karmic work is finished. They're so old and insignificant that they're long forgotten until something is triggered; or they represent some piece of the past that we've moved on from enough that has no bearing on our current circumstances; or they do not match who we've become energetically, in which case, we have to find the light within that particular piece.

To come into our wisdom, we must first find the courage to be ourselves, and to find courage requires releasing our egos. If we wish to create a new world based on values that respect our individual freedoms and allow us the space to live our purpose, we cannot hold on to 3D. It doesn't work. It's what we've been seeing for the past several years. Whether it be in the ways we hold Otherness within and without, or how we apply established societal norms and perpetuate our feelings of worthlessness, we are constantly at odds with how to be our best divine selves while trying to prove that we are the best.

There is no room for the Divine in our 3D standards of perfection. We are wired for judgment. We can easily become disempowered, fearful, and ignorant of who we are and what we want because our identity has been co-opted by a powerful parent, teacher, or caregiver, as well as the shitty 3D environment that surrounds us.

This has to do, in part, with the fact that most of our human existence in 3D involves being enslaved to a system. Most of us don't know who we really are apart from our identities in Separation. When we try to redefine 3D, we end up in the same place where no meaningful change takes place, leading to greater frustration and a tendency to blame the institutions for failing us. Thus, we remain stuck—accepting our shitty or could-be-shittier position but never really experiencing any true happiness, peace, or bliss.

We've been unraveling our Separation identities to come into our divine identities, which has led to an identity crisis of mass proportions. From our relationships falling apart to our increasing dissatisfaction with work or our sense of purposelessness to our feelings of hopelessness, we've been cracking under the weight of expectation and loss. Very little about our lives reflects what we hope they'd be, and while it may be a welcome, if not an exciting, change for some, it's absolutely terrifying for most.

Yet, in Oneness, we are the primary factor of the equation. We are the way in which evil can be eradicated; we just need to understand its true nature to figure out how. It certainly isn't by perpetuating Separation and focusing on being virtuous because the very rules of Separation teach us that doing so keeps polarity in place.

We spend a good portion of our young lives being labeled and allowing those labels to define us, only to spend an equal amount of time in therapy or in dysfunctional experiences trying to break out of them. We've been tethered to the world of 3D consciousness that laid before us very simple rules and practices for success and happiness, only to discover that those rules and practices have contributed to this early-life crisis.

Oneness reinforces that accepting ourselves as we are and recognizing our own divinity and power is the only way to end Separation—and thus kill the evil that is born from fear. Oneness consciousness, where everything is literally at One, throws polarity out the window. Good and evil don't exist in a world absent of judgment. They are merely two sides of the same coin that serve as the currency in Separation.

That's how all those pieces of light that can't survive Separation find their way back into our lives. It could be that our goofy or cynical sides give us the humor and insight we lost along the way. We might even heal our relationships that have long suffered now that we can own who we are and be fully present. We won't know until we begin the process; and while it starts with our karmic story being made whole, it takes a while to find a resolution.

Stop Crying Your Heart Out
Rhea

The karmic undoing process provides us with the foundations of our lives. That is why these books have not been prescriptive, and whilst peppered with my stories, they have not always gone into as much detail as many would have preferred. It's not because of some cop-out on our part, nor is it to protect myself from the epically cringe moments in which I was a willing or an unwilling participant. It's because it's not up to anyone else to speak our intuition, and often, when we focus on someone else's story, we don't see the nuances in our own.

That is what we are left with today when it comes to most spiritual modalities. Whether it's that the practitioners don't understand the theory that underpins the processes or whether it's easier to focus on the tangible steps to service as many clients as possible, we miss the *why* when focusing on the *how*. In doing so, we inhibit the meaningful changes that we so desperately want.

Ultimately, we are looking for our power. In every situation where we are hurt, bereft, sad, or feeling like we're on the losing side of life, we're facing our perceived powerlessness. The problem is when we turn to something else outside of us to deliver it back to us, regardless of whether it's another person in the form of a lover, teacher, or acolyte, we compound the issue rather than release it. We cannot ask anyone to give us back the power we lost, and even if they seem to do so, there will inevitably come a time when we end up back where we started.

That's the thing about the fall. We only fall because we aren't seeing who we really are or our lives for what they really are. Instead, we willfully lie to ourselves about how we cannot dictate our own lives and what's possible for us—we allow others to put their Shit onto us, and we wear it like it's a vintage designer jacket we got for the bargain price of our life force.

When we measure our choices based on what we think the consequences are, we lose the point of this endeavor, which is to remind ourselves that we are in the driver's seat of our lives. It doesn't matter what the outcome is; it's the process of coming to a choice that often is the most valuable. We are, in some cases for the first time, listening to ourselves and doing what we want to do rather than abandoning ourselves for some future idea. We are building trust in ourselves so that we can decide our own lives, we are tapping into the knowing that our lives can be better than what we're currently experiencing, we're creating the opportunities for our hope to be realized, and we're having the faith to see it through. That is huge. It's also the underpinnings of Love.

Love, the topic that I cannot stop talking about, is the connection we cultivate within ourselves that allows us to walk through the world as who we are rather than who we think we need to be. It allows for what comes next. When we make choices with trust, faith, hope, and knowing, we connect to our power. The power to decide what is best for us becomes front and center in our lives, and we facilitate the possibility that we can get what we desire without settling.

I could bang on about how I wasn't in any kind of relationship when I was contorting myself or how I couldn't see my divinity when I allowed someone else to define it for me. But we're meant to deepen our understanding as we progress, not stay stuck in the same place. We also cannot continue to reference our pasts to show how far we've come. We will always be beholden to them, despite how much we evidence otherwise.

That's what it means to settle. It's not dating some guy who doesn't pick up the tab, working for less pay than we want, or even having a lackluster meditation session and going back for more. Those are just socially constructed forms of settling that focus on the byproduct of the action rather than the action itself. Settling is not allowing ourselves to even sit at the table—to deny a part of us to placate another person or idea and then wonder why things feel a little less fulfilled than we'd like them to.

We aren't settling for someone else, we are settling for a version of ourselves. We are allowing the misinformed, misshapen, and misunderstood illusions of our power to limit what is possible for our lives because we aren't clear on how powerful we really are. Our choices themselves are not what makes us powerful; neither is acknowledging that we have the power to choose—those are merely the steps we take to get to the place where we can understand where our power starts. The only way we can understand where our power can go and what it can do is to let those choices unfold—not in the short term but as we continue to live our lives. At some point, we will see that they always had a point, and that point was always Love.

Stand By Me

When we constantly look outside of ourselves, we miss all the ways we have actually shown up for what we want. We compound the lie that we are powerless to create our own lives in a way that makes sense to us. We eventually lose ourselves to the point that we can't see a hope in hell of coming back.

When I look back at my life in my karma, I see a lot of pain, confusion, and telling myself that I need to stop dreaming and accept my fate. But now I see that the one thing that I was denying was my fate. By allowing others to tell me what I was here for, what I needed to accept, and what my life was going to look like, I allowed them to tell me what my fate should be. In doing so, I turned myself into a cautionary tale.

And I was a goddamn cautionary tale—the person who came into this world with so much light and power and who allowed someone else's Shit to tell her she didn't have any. I allowed a system of oppression, judgment, and shame to dictate my worth. In doing so, I took all that power and used it against myself, muting my light in the process. I may have known that Love was one of the most important things that I could wield, but I allowed myself to forget it until all I could do was scream "Fuck This" until I lost my voice.

Except I didn't lose my voice at all. I finally remembered that I had one. In every moment where I decided that I was worth listening to and acted accordingly, I saw who I was. I picked up all the pieces of myself that I had discarded, and I reunited myself to the point that I could see my power again. My power was how I could change my world and then live in it.

That's why in *A Karmic Affair*, I ended the book by saying that we need to show up for ourselves. We've spent so long hiding who we are under the guise of societal programming, obligations, or just general pack mentality that we've forgotten the pack is fucking miserable (apart from a select few who are profiting off our misery). Instead, we buy into the superficial projections and strive for unattainable goals whilst telling ourselves that this is what success means.

What Shit—and it really is. All of it. We start our lives as light, then we give it away to the structures that tell us we shouldn't have any. We relegate our fate to hell and serve each other substandard meals whilst looking for the Michelin star. But we can't blame the structures for making us miserable. We're the ones who listen to them.

We also can't blame ourselves; we didn't know any better. I allowed my Love for connection to disconnect me from everything that ever mattered. I lost myself and the ability to share that self with another—along with any chance of connecting to something larger than me. But I didn't need to be silent, I just needed to see that it was all Shit.

The rules. The constructs. The expectations. The very way our society has been structured reinforces that separation within. I wouldn't be able to remain whole in a world that was so upside-down it was distorted, and I wouldn't believe I was powerful in a world that told me that I could never have any power.

There was never going to be a way to hold on to Love, not when the world was set up to ensure that I had to extinguish my light to survive it. I may have been the common denominator in all of my experiences and the main character in my story, but that doesn't mean I was to blame for my choices when I believed the world wasn't built for me. I was simply trying to survive it whilst waiting for the next fall to remind me that the odds weren't ever going to be in my favor.

Now, I'm not eschewing responsibility for my role in all of my Shit. When we excuse our mistakes to show that we have no hope of doing better, we lose trust in ourselves to create a different reality, we diminish our knowing, and we put our faith in others just so we don't have to have any faith in ourselves. But we do need to accept that the world wasn't built for us, and it never will be unless we build it for ourselves.

That's where our responsibility truly lies. If we want better, we have to do better and make it better for us. If we cannot have faith in ourselves, then we can't really change anything—especially as faith is the bridge between who we are today and who we can really be.

I wasn't just experiencing my fears when I was down my spiritual k-hole. I was showing myself that I was capable of moving forward and keeping going when it mattered. I was also showing myself that not only could I take responsibility for my life, but I could also take responsibility for my healing. Eventually, I realized that none of the Shit I'd been wading in was mine.

Much like getting to the end of this book, it took time before I realized all of it was an illusion and the problem wasn't me. There had never been anything wrong with me, and that belief was the only issue standing in my way. I could do anything that I set my heart to, and the only difference between my karmic life and my post-karmic one was that I did it rather than pretending it was impossible.

If we keep ourselves stuck in a never-ending cycle of self-improvement, we'll never see that 3D is the problem, and all of our efforts will be fruitless. We will still look to someone or something else to tell us what to do, say, or ask to be happy. But we can't fuck up, as much as Separation wants us to believe it's possible. Eventually, we'll be ready to see that we're not only responsible for our lives but also that we can make them happen.

We are all perfectly us, and on some level, we know it. Otherwise, we wouldn't be here, living, creating, fucking, and working our asses off for better days. Thing is, we've told ourselves that those better days are ahead of us, that we have to prove we are worthy of them, and that they can be taken away from us if we fuck up along the way.

We've allowed ourselves to think that it's as good as it can ever be whilst denying ourselves the opportunity to discover that it gets a whole load better. But if we allow our highest expression to be our guiding force, we can bring that expression to life. To realize it, we just need to take step after step in Love. That's when all the wisdom we gain throughout our adventures will make sense, and we'll see who we were always meant to be—a loving embodiment of our happiness.

Redemption Song
Liz

Many motivational and holistic coaches have said that if we don't put ourselves first or prioritize ourselves, it's because we don't feel we deserve it. Whether it be that awesome job, fantastic relationship, or dollars in our bank account, we're only one step away from having whatever will make us happy—and that is a matter of deservingness. What they don't understand is that there are six other karmic themes available.

To be fair, at the root of these issues is the core fear *I Am not Good Enough*, but if we cannot recognize what's driving it and how the story is really playing out for us, no amount of journaling, listing, breathing, or inspirational posts will manifest the reality we're meant to have. This is why it's truly disappointing when spiritual influencers sell feel-good methods to their followers that really don't lead to any meaningful change in their lives.

Spirituality cannot be simplified or distilled into a notion of deserving—especially when we're so disconnected from ourselves that we equate deservingness with entitlement or the sum total of efforts put into proving ourselves at any given turn. I did X, so I deserve Y—or even more martyry; I didn't do X, so I definitely deserve

Y as my redemption. However we spin it, the idea that we aren't deserving of anything, is merely a smokescreen for the deep-seated fear that we are not *good enough* for all the beauty and Love that we can afford ourselves.

It's a lie. All of it. Yet, shame, the belief that we'll never be *good enough*, keeps us in the nearly indestructible loop of Separation and 3D consciousness. To have anything or everything we want, we cannot possibly be ourselves. Instead, what we receive is bestowed or endowed upon us, granted by a genie (if we can be clever enough to couch all our wishes into three requests to have it all, such as "I wish for 100 more wishes").

All these coaches feed into it time and again, selling us pithy quotes and half-assed solutions to a very simple, albeit painful, issue. We've forgotten who we are and that we are powerful enough to grasp that we are deserving, lovable, worthy, enough, whole, good, and perfect.

We don't need to convince ourselves otherwise, nor can we choose to believe something if we cannot fundamentally connect to that truth. That's what all these self-appointed healers cannot get us to do, despite how well-intentioned they might be. To know the truth about ourselves, to recognize that light, that Love inside all of us, we must remember who we are. That is all.

It's not easy, but it's so very simple because it speaks to the most basic knowing in our hearts—a knowing that Rhea mentions early on in this book, and something she didn't doubt until she was old enough to internalize the oft-perpetuated message that Love is for chumps and settling is the only way through.

A new life, a new world, and a greater potential rest within all of us when we stop buying into that lie and start listening to ourselves. It begins when we stop being sold the message of our disempowerment. If the root of our issues is really that we're all so "undeserving" and that it can be easily remedied like a light switch turning on a new belief system, we wouldn't continue to suffer under the weight of our issues while turning over our hard-earned money to others to tell us what's wrong with us.

We're not unlovable. We're not unworthy. We're not nothing. We're not evil. We're not imperfect. We're not broken. And we are most certainly not undeserving. Deep down, in our core, we know we are *good enough*, but we need to shine the light inward to see that truth for ourselves. No one else can shine it for us, nor can they bring us to our own redemption. Only we can do that for ourselves when we connect to the power that we so readily surrender to others.

There's no room for this anymore. We cannot look outside for the answers and solutions to what ails us. No partner, friend, coach, mentor, or guide can do it for us, either. We're timing out on our capacity to seek assistance from others, and frankly, it's about time. Otherwise, our dependence will keep us locked in a state of Separation from ourselves.

It's not the time to panic, either. We all have the ability to get ourselves there, like Rhea did. Despite what she tells anyone about how much I helped her, I really didn't. All I had to do was keep reminding her that she could tackle her Shit on her own and that she had all the answers she needed. Although, with Rhea, there's never really any answer that can satisfy her unless it comes from her. At this point, her favorite phrase is, "I was right." Maybe you can call me her spiritual cheerleader. That's way more fun than a spiritual counselor.

Always On The Run

Until we figure out what it takes to come into our power and be fully responsible agents of our lives, we will be reminded of our powerlessness. It can be frustrating to the point that we'd love to give up, forget that we ever started this path, and wish to go back to the beginning.

As Rhea mentioned in an earlier chapter, "I did it for you" became my mantra whereby everything I did was for my husband, my children, or something external. Unfortunately, little by little, who I was and what I was here for fell by the wayside.

That's the thing about life in 3D. When we're separate from ourselves, life in 3D is unbearable, so our raison d'être often lies outside of ourselves. To sacrifice is noble, to put ourselves last is selfless, and to put our care on display is virtuous. We are molded to believe that outward acts of "kindness" and "compassion" speak our goodness to the world, but we actually forget who we're really doing anything for, and that is really us.

A part of me felt incapable of defining my life. It can be terrifying to think we're responsible for bringing that amazing person to life (see why Rhea wanted to kill me or the Guides at times?). Even when we approach our purpose or mission work, we could just as well make it about others and turn ourselves into sacrificial lambs. Perhaps, if it weren't for my karmic story, I wouldn't have settled for what seemed enough at the time, yet I didn't believe I had other options. I let one choice lead me to the next until I felt trapped under a host of consequences I didn't think I was capable of handling. Unlike Rhea, however, I couldn't "Fuck This" out of my life. I had a spouse and two children relying on me. In my case, it took untangling myself from the daily dregs and humdrum pattern of the stay-at-home life.

So, I refocused my priorities. While keeping my family at the top, I inched my way back to join them. I started seeing clients and started to write. Writing brought such a light to my life that I kept going, even if no one would see the end result; what mattered was the passion and commitment it pulled out of me. Even though I always felt a calling when it came to my spiritual practice, writing became my religion.

When I clawed back those words, "I did it for you," one book at a time, one session at a time, one hour of alone time, I saw all that I had forgotten. For as much as I was doing for others, I slowly had to recognize that I was doing it for myself, too. I was happiest when I could be useful, which required me to be in my power. But I needed to add myself back into the equation to do so. Like a person having to prove their gifts or abilities to someone else to determine exactly how "real" they are, I was only going to make a difference when I could show myself that I mattered to me.

That's what makes us real to ourselves and the world. When we prioritize ourselves enough, we can exist fully, with two feet in our realities. Otherwise, we exist for others, which means we remain split in our worlds, where a part goes to one person, another to work, and perhaps another to the cause we lend ourselves to on a Sunday. None of it is real unless we can fully connect ourselves to it, which takes being fully embedded in ourselves, otherwise we render our lives and whatever we touch meaningless. This, in turn, makes us disposable—just another body or person in the already weak link holding up the tentpoles.

What a difference it makes, though, to hold ourselves up fully, thereby holding up our purpose, living it fully, and integrating it into our lives. It took fifteen years for me to come into this, to understand on every level of my being how to live and own every step, project, relationship, and word. As Rhea says, it's responsibility. For me, however, it's more than that—it's divine power.

Divine power is the combination of three features that elevate human life beyond comprehension, especially when we've been burdened by our karma. The first is purpose. When we're in a position to serve the whole, it means we understand how to best serve ourselves. This shows up in the form of living consciously every day. The second is Love. When we shine our light, everything is illuminated, and nothing can possibly live in the dark. To shine our light is to embrace all that this life has to offer (this precludes any judgment; when we say "all" we mean all). The third is integrity. To have integrity is to be fully aligned in all bodies, conscious, awake, and living our purpose or mission to the best of our ability, without shirking from the responsibilities they entail.

What's Up?
Rhea

When I started the podcast, many people I knew believed that anything spiritual was slightly crazy. I was told to keep it to myself, asked if I wanted to go public on a podcast with someone who said they spoke to Angels, and it was heavily hinted that a safe place for my crystals should be a drawer or the back of a cupboard. It felt like I was in a secret society where "believers" would drop a phrase or two over a dinner table and hope that the person sitting across from them would light up. And if they didn't… then both parties could just pretend nothing was ever mentioned.

I approached meeting new people carrying the stress of how or when I should casually drop in my beliefs into the conversation—especially given that the first thing people tend to ask is what our jobs are. I diluted the truth to make it palatable and glossed over the work so I wouldn't seem unhinged. But, when I went full throttle, I met one of four reactions:

1. Interest: Asking about the work and telling me about their experiences and beliefs regarding what I shared.

2. Slightly Combative Interest: Asking about the work and then telling me about other spiritual theories that made more sense than mine.
3. Just Combative: Asking about the work and then trying to prove to me that spirituality was nonsense.
4. Silence: Wondering if they didn't ask further questions, maybe I'd just go away.

For those who were quick to dismiss spirituality, there were plenty of reasons to do so, whether or not I agreed with them. Firstly, the realms of spirituality are so wide, and like anything else, the outliers define the mainstream. The theories on lizards, body snatchers, and evil forces akin to a Marvel superhero movie come off so far-fetched that they taint anything that isn't perceived as rational.

As a result, many of us have to bear other people's opinions in mind when owning ourselves and deciding what information to share, unless we could be sure that by the end of the conversation, they agreed (or kind of agreed) with our point of view. Whether it's hearing voices, being psychic, using a pendulum, staring into a crystal ball, shuffling cards, or any practice that involved communicating with the unseen world, admitting that these things could be real insinuated that our grasp on reality was not.

If we do the work and it works, we recount our story in the hope that by telling someone how great we are, they'll feel great about us, too. And, if the work doesn't work (because we don't get the thing we wanted, we don't want to actually face our Shit, or untangling our constructed lives to create our own is a bit too messy), we conclude that spirituality is frivolous and a waste of time. We also have to make sure that we appear to be the people who we've always been or happier in a quantifiable way. Otherwise, it's all bollocks.

To sidestep that often very uncomfortable fact, one has to prove that their life is better than someone else's—partly to justify their beliefs to others, but mostly to justify their beliefs to themselves. There has to be a reason that isn't just attributed to the stars but also why they're here, how important they are, and what they are going to get for it—especially when they've spent so much time and money finding out what their akashic records revealed.

Evidently, there's something to be said for spiritual work. Aside from the obvious impact it's had on my life, it's pretty clear from where I'm standing (no longer lying prostrate on the ground from my emotional devastation) that when practiced with integrity, it can help heal a lot of our Shit.

But there is a drawback to spirituality that I couldn't quite shake when having these types of conversations, regardless of who was doing the majority of the talking and whose voice was loudest. It seemed that most of the people who "received downloads" or "aggressively detached all the way to enlightenment" had folded their spirituality into their identity to the point they used it to validate their worth. That meant the biggest side effect of taking the spirituality pill was that it made some people (including myself, at times) a little preachy.

You Wish

Spirituality was being used as another way to define ourselves and our place in the world. People were Starseeds, Indigos, or crystals. They were teachers, influencers, yogis, gurus or shamans. They were psychic, intuitive, reincarnated Cleopatras, or a special kind of channel who had a seat at the Intergalactic Chamber of Secrets.

To be spiritual meant that we should look, act, speak, and believe a certain way. Moving from one dimension to another became the rebranded heaven and hell, where being *good enough* ensured we got there, whereas having a drink, shopping at a chain store, and topping the day off with a one-night stand was the surefire way to ensure that we wouldn't.

For a practice of non-judgment and shame, there was a fuck-ton of both; and for a group of people who believed they were on Earth to end Separation and encourage harmony, there were lots of labels and disdain. After all, there was a fight between light and dark, of which we were all soldiers, and we all had our part to play.

When it came to the whole "3D" versus "5D" war (and I say both those words very deliberately because it was often made to feel like some kind of battle), it was even messier. There was no room for a dissenting opinion. Instead, it was "wrong" and "evil," and the person who held it didn't matter or needed to be converted. 5D was this standard of perfection in the lifestyle, character, and state of the world. It was a goal that we had to get to and then obviously tell everyone else whilst secretly judging everyone else who hadn't.

I don't know about you, but to me, that sounds awfully similar to everything we've seen before whilst preaching that it's different—waiting to be proven right, relishing in the demise of someone else, turning everything into a story to explain the fear and powerlessness, and then throwing out every excuse in the book as to why it isn't working out whilst waiting for the promised land. It also sounds a lot like karma.

That is where karma becomes a bitch. Not because it is one, but because it's being seen as outside of ourselves: punishing and debilitating our power until we're subservient, rebellious, or Shit scared. Rather than becoming the most powerful versions of ourselves, we remain powerless whilst constantly saging each other, thanking something bigger, or berating ourselves.

It takes courage to admit things aren't going great. In recognizing that things can get better, we give ourselves a chance to make it real. But when we perpetuate our stories of powerlessness under a different guise, we trade our autonomy for compliance and miss the opportunity for change. And when we take advantage of other people's will to make a better life by imposing our half-baked insights into their lives, we risk hurting them whilst telling ourselves that we're changing the world, one person at a time.

If we approach spirituality from a place of entitlement, fear, or absolute authority evidenced by ego-inspired life hacks, we perpetuate our ignorance whilst keeping those we're trying to help stuck in the very place they're trying to escape. It takes the darkest part of spirituality and twists it, so that anyone who could be helped, inspired, or even empowered by the wisdom that some of the words can offer either turns away entirely or loses all trust in themselves and the light.

They can't see that those words have been warped to the point that they've lost their original meaning; they can't see that the practitioner often doesn't understand what they are repeating and can't see a way through. So, instead of people finding their light, it gets snuffed out, and humanity loses another chance for redemption.

Moreover, if we approach spirituality from a place of powerlessness, we give up our agency. It's not, nor can it ever be, a substitute for our own power. Nor is it a method to get that one thing that has otherwise eluded us, or a one-size-fits-all delivery service to relieve our FOMO. It's also not a badge of honor, a label, or a way to martyr ourselves on the altar of some twisted reflection of our purpose.

We don't have to manifest a better life or surrender until we can't see who we are anymore. We're meant to grow up and take responsibility for our lives. If we rely on others to give us permission or give us a reason, we won't find anything other than a deflated life jacket. We will keep trying to fill it with hot air whilst wondering why we aren't ascending to the promised land that others keep rubbing in our faces over a glass of champagne. We may also not notice that they can afford the champagne because they've convinced a sea of lost souls to hand over their hard-earned money in exchange for a chance to run a successful coaching business that doesn't coach anything other than how to get the next bunch of people to do the same.

Spirituality isn't the gift we share with the world, it is a path to discover our gifts—that, when embraced, have the capacity to change the world. Whilst my life may feel like a miracle, and whilst spirituality may have helped facilitate that, I made the choices for myself. Even though spiritual work is one of the most magical and beautiful things I've ever explored, it's only because it allowed me to acknowledge what I really wanted and what I was capable of achieving when I connected to myself.

Perfect
Liz

We didn't come into body to fall in love—at least, not in the way that Separation consciousness portrays love. That simpering savior syndrome masked as our One true love was merely a way for the ego to find comfort in a world where Separation and free will reigned. By focusing our energies on the pursuit of someone to save us from the overwhelming 3D life, we could at least be assured that we wouldn't have to weather life alone, nor would we have to exist in the uncertainty that we aren't acceptable for partnership, which was how we could exist in wholeness in the face of Separation.

The Divine is perfect. Our souls know this because, as emanations of the Divine, each one is a unique expression of the Divine. A bit like when a child wants to emulate a parent, we admire and only see their perfection to such an extent that we want to be like the Divine and do everything like the Divine. This is where the comparison stops because when a soul is in human body, it cannot be exactly like the Divine since the physical body is limited in the temporal world. Yet, moving into Oneness means that we're supposed to be moving closer to, not further from, our divine selves. This requires accepting our inherent perfection while living in a world dominated by Otherness, division, and the shame that results when we believe that we are not measuring up.

Our core fear that we are not *good enough* can easily feed into these feelings and contribute to our karmic story. However, even if we've divested enough or all of our karma, we may still hold remnants of fear, which are underscored by the deep doubts and insecurities that informed our karmic story. These fears are not about whether we are *good enough*; rather, they speak to how we doubt our divine perfection. So, while we may grasp that we are *good enough*, we still fall short of perfection.

Our narrow view of perfection stems from just one thing: self-judgment. That self-judgment applies the belief that *I Am only Worthy if I Am* _____. What fills in the blank depends on three things:

1. Established social standards which manage to prevail because of the stories we internalize and perpetuate throughout our various relationships. These do not start out being about how we see ourselves, but about our world that will only deem us worthy *if…*

2. How we understand love. Not in the big "L" word that we discuss in pretty much every book, but in the lowercase "l". Our need to feel something akin to connection, to be supported and feel whole, will have us desperate to fill a void, even if it means creating a false connection to anything

that doesn't make us feel like a failure. So, we will contort and distort our perfection to seem perfect and, therefore, worthy in the eyes of someone else.

3. Hope. Not one of the four pillars which expresses our deepest heart's desires, but the lowercase "h", the kind of desperate, hopeful need that we project out into the world that someone will save us from ourselves. If someone else decides that we matter, then we will know that we are worthy.

It is challenging, if not virtually impossible, to realize our perfection when we are battling what we perceive as our failings in our eyes, which we then project onto others. Even for the karma-less, if we haven't had a dose of humility or been able to work with self-acceptance, we can still struggle with the simple concepts of Otherness until we finally have that come-to-Jesus moment that says: *I Am Who I Am*.

Owning who we are is the most divine act we can ever commit. It is truly what makes us that badass who is able to hold ourselves and others in compassion. To say *I Am Who I Am* doesn't mean that we are fixed, static creatures incapable of change, growth, or evolution. Rather, it recognizes that we can only fully grow and evolve when we can truly accept who we are first and foremost, which is the Divine. When we accept that we are the Divine, we can step fully into our fate because that's when we realize that we have the capacity to uncover our power and realize our perfection—by fully, completely, totally, and utterly accepting that our present self is a result of our past self—and make our peace with that.

We cannot do this just through the mind. Mindfulness teachers may want us to believe we can. To a certain degree, possibly. Our mental bodies are so powerful that we can certainly reconcile our worldview and self-view and somehow fit them together and make it seem like we can accept everything. Yet, all of our bodies need to be on board and steering this ship together. So, if we're holding an insecurity or doubt in one of those bodies, the mental body alone cannot get us there.

Oneness demands wholeness. It requires not only full-body consciousness where all of our bodies are aligned but also for us to be turned towards a path to higher consciousness. We cannot rely solely on our mental body just as much as we cannot rely on our emotional one to carry the weight of our Separation issues. Although, there are enough New Age spiritual teachers and influencers who will have us believe this is the way, and they are very convincing. The jargon, the seeming simplicity of their approach (make a list, check it twice, everything is a test, love yourself first, let go of your small self) can often sound good, and the results (at least their own) appear amazing.

We might tell ourselves that we want that. They may convince us that we can have it. And we just might be able to… to a point. But no one else's success can be matched by another's, just as no one else's personal growth can compare to anyone else's.

We all have our own paths, our own gifts, our own talents, and our own fate. So any time we try someone else's methodology or secret and apply it to our own, it often doesn't work enough or at all. It's not due to anything else (like us not working at it hard enough), it's due to the fact that our own healing has to be directed by ourselves.

When we do anything from our spiritual bodies, our growth and evolution happen much more quickly. Yet, being *the* best as opposed to being *our* best doesn't allow us to grow or evolve. On the contrary, it stunts our growth because then we have nowhere to go. We've done it all, been it all, said it all, and the Divine didn't come for a party of one.

Sweetheart

We go without love in 5D so that we can live in Love. We cannot keep settling for one thing and then expect the real ideal to show up and replace it. We have to make room for it first. That's what this 5D transition period is for—to make room. And we make room by eliminating what isn't working. So whatever governed 3D (easy answer, Separation) must go—and along with it, everything that supported Separation, no matter how well-intentioned it may be.

Our relationships are one of the primary ways we move along our fate because they keep us in touch with love. But believing that relationships are the *alpha* and *omega* of our lives, we have sold our fates short. We have not been able to completely realize who we are. Instead, we get caught up in the years of searching and settling together and joining the hamster wheel of brunches, marriage, children, and retirement. We've allowed ourselves to be so consumed by relationships and the ins and outs of getting together and breaking up that we haven't come up for air long enough to see that we're not living our lives or fulfilling our fate.

We've been living in a 3D fantasy world, but we cannot afford to be any longer. We've been stuck for far too long in a world that we can no longer support, just as it can no longer support us. The wells have run dry. We are the ones now responsible for our well-being, and we have been waiting for this day. As unprepared as many of us have found ourselves to be, we don't need much more than we already have to get ready. There is pretty much nothing from 3D that can make this leap into 5D. We just have to be prepared for what lies ahead.

This isn't easy. We are the kings of excuses and queens of exit strategies. There isn't a single thing we can't Houdini our way out of if it suits us. We are inclined to fill the vacuum. We cannot stand space. Humans love distractions and easy fixes. They want leaders who will promise anything and throw out crumbs. They want relationships but settle for situationships since something is always better than nothing in 3D.

Separation has become so firmly embedded in our consciousness that eliminating it is really heartbreaking work. It's the kind of work that demands we break ourselves open to see the Divine. Yet, we don't necessarily heal the heartbreak through our karmic story. Some might, but the reality is that we can carry around this broken-hearted experience even after our karma. It may not define our lives as much as when we were in our karmic story and may not feel so important when we're feeling fearless and able to dismiss our ego needs. However, being fearless is not the same as having courage, and our hearts do not automatically heal the moment we put the final nail in the coffin of our karmic story.

It is not that simple because when we lived in Separation *and* without a direct connection to Source, we always had holes in our hearts and depended on something else to fill them… until now. 5D allows for everything to exist without Separation, which is why we could never fully resolve the broken heart syndrome until we could end Separation and come into complete wholeness in every area of our lives.

We need two other key pieces to fall into place to heal our broken hearts. The first is to recognize that it's always been there. Lifetime after lifetime, we have lived with the challenge of carrying a broken heart. And when we have a broken heart, everything we do can only be half-hearted, which is why lifetime after lifetime has been burdened with a sense of unmet longing and unfinished business. The second is to accept that this has helped shape humankind's evolution or lack thereof. A broken heart informs a person's experience in three possible ways:

1. Compels them to pursue work/projects/ideas that never really pan out.
2. Convinces them that materiality is all that matters.
3. Affirms that everything they encounter is a measure of their woundedness.

Yet, if we keep settling, we won't allow the one thing that we need to make room for Oneness, that is Love. Through Love, we not only own our most divine selves but infuse all we are, say, and do with Love. Understanding this to our very core is what gets us from Separation to Oneness. That's when free will dissolves—it cannot hold the experience of Oneness. So, when we are able to share Love with others, we are bringing the Divine into our everyday lives, which is precisely how the world will be able to shift consciousness.

The Way We Were
Rhea

We might think that once we are out of our karma, have settled our ego, and burned out our core fear that relationships would no longer be an issue. However, we can still overthink, overplan, and overstress ourselves into our old patterns. Regardless of whether those issues come to fruition (which they often don't), we can still torture ourselves with our history and make it seem real even if it isn't.

Separation, at its core, is a very defensive place to be. We want to wear the rosy glasses, but they've already been stolen, trampled on, and thrown into the waste disposal. Whilst we want to be happy, it might not seem possible if all we've ever known was life in karma. So, even though we may have reached full consciousness and even higher consciousness, we may not feel like we can live our lives without a fight—especially since so many people around us are still fully embedded in Separation.

For me, there was more than that. I was also secretly addicted to my own doom. I had learnt in pain, I had overcome my pain, and a small part of me was curious if the pain would resurface. I almost couldn't help it. I looked for problems because I didn't believe new experiences would show up. I wanted to test how strong the karmic undoing process really was because I couldn't fully trust it was all over.

In some way or another, many of us are addicted to our own doom. Closing one chapter and starting another is one of the scariest things a human can do. Not only because it is uncertain but also because there is a sense of grief that many of us don't want to face. Let's be frank: as humans, we hate endings because they remind us of the big endings that we don't want to deal with. We've fallen too many times to even hope that we won't fall again.

It's the heartbreak we replay throughout our lives. Not only does it reinforce Separation, but it also ensures we don't ever feel we can be whole-hearted again. There are too many unhappy people in this world to believe it could be different for us, and our personal histories echo that belief. That's why, to heal that part of us that is addicted to our own doom, we have to heal the very idea that we are only here to suffer and that the world is out to get us, so we must guard against it.

That's a monumental challenge. In one way or another, most of us skirt the edges of endings all the time, avoiding them out of fear but toying with them out of some warped sense of indestructibility. We allow our minds to create worst-case scenarios, so that we know we are prepared for it, whilst reassuring ourselves we will be fine if our desires don't materialize. We seek protection from the seemingly inevitable heartbreak, so we can avoid being hurt again.

I secretly reveled in the personal torture because it reinforced the idea that I did something wrong. That habit, that addiction, and that blame was the only way I could control my pain, which meant I stood a chance of fixing it. Past lovers replayed in my head like a bad romantic comedy, lessons I'd learnt became warning signs, and I rejected what I wanted by telling myself it could never happen. I may have been courageous to see past my broken heart, but that didn't mean that I wasn't still living with it.

To be fair, very few of us know what it is like to live in a world without Separation. It's hard to find our power and even harder to hold on to it. Even if we can bring our own world into harmony, engaging with the wider world almost ensures that Separation informs a part of our lives. It's understandable to want to protect ourselves from it, to wonder whether we will still be affected by it, or to preempt a losing battle and give up before we are forced to. But in doing so, we don't give ourselves the chance to see how far our power can reach and what it can do.

Throughout the podcast, I've explained that "experience makes normal." As we change our perspective, it becomes natural, and we wire in a new way of being. I have also explained that we do not shift our world overnight but build it step by step. However, whilst we can evidence all the change around us, without bringing our power front and center, we cannot fully embed ourselves into our new reality.

When we doubt whether our power will work, we search for exit strategies with minimal fallout. Or, we quite simply use one of the many excuses we employed in our karma (which ultimately boils down to it isn't meant to be). We keep one foot in our old world whilst trying to take a leap with the other—stretching ourselves to the point we feel like we might break in half. But when we are unwilling to take a risk on ourselves, the product of our efforts falls like a house of cards. Every brick becomes paper thin and is easily toppled over by an errant gust of wind. And all the Trust we've cultivated becomes a liability rather than a guiding force.

It's easy to say that to heal our hearts, we have to go back to the first memory we have of this lifetime and go from there—to have compassion for the person we were, to let it go, to manifest a better one, or thank our lucky stars for all the silver linings. But when the root cause of our issue isn't a specific moment but a series of them that stem from a world set up to muffle our power, we can get lost in the self-absorption of it all, ignore it, or look for someone else to kiss it and make it better.

I wasn't the one to break my heart, nor had it been broken in one fell swoop. Rather, it was in a series of small breaks, little betrayals, disappointments, and unmet expectations along the way. And whilst I'd always known and believed in Love, that Love had become distorted once I lost faith in it, leaving the rest of the pillars to crumble.

What's Love Got To Do With It?

In a twist of fate, I was also addicted to love. My search for love was a bid to replace the Love I believed I had lost, and it reconnected me to Love. Every person who crossed my path pointed me back to myself, and I remembered who I was. That meant that as much as the world had hurt me, it also had provided the exact tools to transcend the Shit experience. The only difference was my approach and perspective.

Even though the karmic undoing process allowed me to restore that Trust within myself, I couldn't extend it. However, nothing was as simple or as black-and-white as I wanted to believe. It never had been. The only difference was whether I was willing to take the risk and listen to myself, no matter what others thought.

To bring our power into our lives, we have to see it first. That is what the karmic process teaches us and why it is a gift that we give ourselves. That is how powerful we are—we made ourselves believe that we were powerless. We bought into Separation, and we chose to perpetuate it.

Our karma will always hit us where it hurts (it would be fairly ineffectual if it didn't). That's partly because that's where we will sit up and take notice of it and partly because it is showing us where the hurt resides so we can heal it. However, when we hold ourselves back from going after what we want in case we still can't get it, we ensure that our lives remain stagnant. We also sacrifice the very desires that pushed us to say "Fuck This" in the first place.

To throw away the potential of our power at the final hurdle is the most heartbreaking act we can do. We break our own hearts again, if only to prove that they had been broken in the past. That's why we are the only ones who can get ourselves out of it and what makes our purpose so significant. It is not only a way to serve others, it is also a way to serve ourselves. Our purpose shows us that we can create in the physical world. Although our purpose is not dependent on another, by anchoring into it, we bring light into our lives and allow that light to extend past us.

We don't need anyone else to write that book, sing that song, or learn that skill. But when we connect to our desires and bring them to fruition, we touch other people. Whether our relationships are more harmonious because we are, or whether we create something that can affect change on a wider scope, we change more than just our world for the better—we change the wider one, too.

Our karma teaches us how to take responsibility for our lives, how to access our inner guidance system, and how to keep going, even when things are pretty dark. It doesn't just give us the tools to come into wholeness within, it also gives us the skills to bring that light into the world.

Had I not taken a chance on myself, I wouldn't have discovered my light again. It took meeting people and saying yes when a part of me wanted to stay home and wait for Prince Charming to knock on my door. But I had to choose to open my door, open my heart, and then open my life to all the possibilities that greeted me. They may have involved other people, but I was the one to facilitate it all. That's why every experience I had throughout my karmic undoing process and after restored the faith I'd abandoned.

When I approached my life from a place of Oneness, all became possible, and I was able to move forward in unexpected and exciting ways. By enabling my full self, I finally experienced what I'd always wanted. I merely needed to see that I had to be the one to not only choose myself but also my fate. That would be how I brought my desires into the physical world and more.

It's Shit to say that we need to find another person to get our lives started. We don't. It's also Shit to say that we don't need anyone, either. It is the very interactions we have with one another that elevate our experience of life—the only difference being whether that experience is one of Separation or harmony. So, the more we come into harmony with ourselves, the more we are able to find those relationships that multiply that harmony out. That is how we create a 5D world, and that is also how we heal our broken hearts. In exercising Love, we heal our own. In bringing Love into all that we do, we heal the world around us, and with Love as our guidance force, we can never break our hearts again.

Walk This Way
Liz

When we're born, the four pillars of Trust form our spiritual foundation. We have them all in spades, so our divine connection (since we haven't been in body for more than a minute) is incredibly strong. Yet, over time, we place trust, faith, and hope in others to tell us what to do and when to expect our lives to begin; we feel incapable of accessing that information ourselves.

Absolutely no psychic, healer, medium, teacher, influencer, oracle card, shaman, or guru will tell us with absolute accuracy what our issue is. Only we can. Perhaps they have enough accuracy to land somewhere near the bullseye, but only we can hit it because the issue lies somewhere within us. Their ability to be near the bullseye depends on three things:

1. Our karma.

If a healer isn't aware of karma or sees it through a particular lens associated with an outdated methodology, they will only be able to read our karmic story. Any advice or wisdom to be gained will be directly related to mitigating or coping with the karma, as opposed to helping to release it or burn it out, which is what's required to move into Oneness. Until that's done, most of what we do, from manifesting or letting go and making lists and "testing" ourselves, will keep us looping through our karma. Our healing work ends up being in service to that karma rather than coming into wholeness.

2. Attachments and energies in our field that block light.

These can influence and hamper what information is coming through and what exactly someone is able to see. Few actually know how to clear a person's auric field permanently in order for meaningful healing to take place. However, when an individual commits to working in the light, experiencing Love, and seeking various methods for raising their vibration, they are less likely to be fully influenced by attachments in their field.

3. Fate.

It may be that we are somewhere along our fate lines that if we are told a particular thing will happen, we could get stalled; often, what allows us to move along the natural unfolding of our lives is our inability to anticipate the next move. A bit like Rhea's story regarding her career path, it was better not knowing some things than predicting every move, since trying to anticipate our next steps causes us to trip over them.

This is why, when we look at spiritual channels, a lot of the work is useless. They tell us their interpretation of our story or what they see in our fields, but they don't have the definitive answer because they cannot be in our bodies, know our history, or read the maps of our souls.

Moreover, no one can prove what's legit and what's not. The lack of trust and the absence of faith push people to test the boundaries of what these spiritual channels might know. As much as people may want to believe, they're inclined not to in the same vein. We can become absolutists demanding proof to believe in something, anything. (Often, everyone wants to know *when* and *how* something might occur, but because of our free will, those are the two things that are often outside of the realm of prediction.) Yet, only we can decide individually what we believe, which isn't easy in a world where "seeing is believing."

There is something way deeper than all the work many of us have explored because when it comes to our souls, the information can only be reached by us. So we dabble and try to find that divine connection through someone else, and sometimes we get close. But our Guides cannot speak to the larger challenge at hand, which is how to commune with our most divine selves to create the lives we want. That, in itself, is truly the challenge for this lifetime.

We've gone so far in the other direction of Oneness that it's taken quite a dysfunctional relationship with spirituality, ourselves, and our Guides to get us to finally say, "Fuck This, I need help." That's what changes the relationship. But we're not really asking for help, we're asking for answers.

Send Me An Angel

Rhea loves to point out that the Guides are imperfect, often wrong, and sometimes just plain annoying. She's owned up to her dependence on New Age spirituality and Guidance; now it's time they own up to why they are an occasional nuisance despite their best intentions.

They don't get it "right" because it's not their job to. While it seems like they set us up for disappointment on occasion, we're not here to get it right, we're here for our growth and evolution. They can't make it "right" for us just so we can bypass the uncomfortable Shit and get to the lesson; often, the lesson comes as we work through our discomfort and misery. We came here to experience Separation and bring Oneness consciousness to this earth plane. Our souls want to do it whether our egos want them to or not. That has been the issue all along—our fucking egos.

All the games, such as "Tell me my future," "Who is my person?" and "Will I be rich, successful, married, have children, live somewhere cool, and be an amazing person?" are all curiosities that feed our disempowerment, and Guidance isn't here for that. Those are left to particular energies or spirits who play in that field of information that serve to bridge our connection to the Divine while in Separation. Yet, in this search for divine connection, we fail to realize that looking outside of ourselves is what keeps us in Separation, and Guidance says, "fuck that."

Humans love ease, and the soul loves peace. Yet, ease and peace are not the same thing. Ease is capitulation; it's the well-worn path of surrender and the path of least resistance. Peace, on the other hand, is represented by the points of light along the way that illuminate our journey. It is the result of the necessary work that comes as we move through our uncomfortable karmic growth periods to reach the various evolutionary goals for our lifetimes.

Peace arises during those moments of our karmic story when we experience healing and wholeness. When we are in peace, while in the throes of our Shit, it points to the way out of our karmic story. The same goes for joy. When we experience those bouts of joy that become cumulative, they don't accumulate and create happiness. They are moments throughout our karmic story that help us realize our purpose.

When we want answers, we want to know what to do or what to expect because we believe ourselves to be powerless to figure it out. Our egos are so consumed with mitigating our fears that they cannot allow us to come to terms with our issue, which can be paralyzing or lead to self-sabotage. So we'll look to anyone who seems to have figured it out, because what we ultimately want is peace in whatever form we can get it.

If seeing a psychic pacifies the sense of powerlessness we're experiencing because we haven't yet met the One, or if we lack the confidence to believe we'll succeed in life, we'll do it because it's better than having to work through all the obstacles standing between us and the actual truth. That truth is that we are powerful and capable beings who are fated for more than the Shit we're experiencing. But we can only realize this when we discern what is standing in our way.

Our unwillingness to see beyond the simple good/evil and God/devil polarity is why 3D consciousness underscores the need to believe that we fall on either side. To be fair, our egos are getting thrown under the bus a lot in this book, but it's about fucking time. They are not us in the larger, most expanded sense of our human identity. They are who we become when our fears rule our lives. They weren't supposed to take over and make the rules. But they did, and that's something we have to unravel along with everything else.

Yet, it's precisely because of our egos that we have a fucked-up, toxic, and co-dependent relationship with our Guides. In seeking to control, anticipate, know, plan, premeditate, and project our future, we have sought answers from mediums, psychics, palm readers, gurus, teachers, influencers, astrologers, and other tools to figure out the "right" steps. But let's face it, if we are in the thick of our karma and in Separation, they can't possibly see the future any better than we can.

This is for two reasons: the first is absolutely nothing can interfere with our primary directive, which is our growth and evolution. Should any information arise that would impede that directive, a veil would be drawn by choice. The second is that our fate is carefully designed by us. To know every step along that path prevents us from realizing our full divine power, which is what is required to create a life full of wisdom, joy and happiness.

Separation prevents us from seeing we are the ones at work, that we are the ones responsible for our fate, and that we are really the ones who have to answer why. Quite frankly, since our own healing can only be designed by us, only we can be the best predictor of our futures because they depend solely on how much of our power we choose to own. But seeing our perfection isn't the end goal of our lives—it's merely the process by which we come into our divinity and exercise it as we grow and evolve.

Guidance is here to accomplish a singular goal: to remind us that we are in charge of our fate. So everything they do, say, convey, teach, show, or share with us is to bring us in line with our most divine selves, to live outside the bounds of our karma—which is the only way to realize our fate and come into our divine power.

All For Love
Rhea

I didn't learn about spirituality by living on a rooftop, chanting and engaging with my visions and the voices in my head. Of course, I did that a bit, but that wasn't where I truly learnt about my divinity. That was where I learnt the theory, which was merely a story until I actually lived it. I learnt about spirituality through my relationships, my passions, and expressing what brought me joy. I learnt about spirituality by seeing myself and living, as opposed to finding an excuse not to.

I also made a friend (which, for Liz, if you know her, is a big deal). For every story or theory that I heard, assimilated, or scoffed at, I had a sounding board and a discussion partner who was always ready to explain to me what she knew. For every issue, question, or recommendation, I had a friend who helped me out. And when she couldn't, I had a whole Guidance Council ready to take the lead to make sure I could understand another side of the story.

But it was only one side of the story. The other side of the story (essentially my story in these books) is how I applied that theory to my own life to truly seal it. I may have remembered that we are all divine through meditation, but I only truly understood it by interacting with others.

For example, my relationship with Liz taught me about what spirituality really meant. Not because she could tell me how many Guides I had, what the Divine Feminine was, and what the Angels can and cannot do but because she gave me the courage to listen to myself. She encouraged me when I intentionally, unintentionally, willingly, and unwillingly put that theory into practice. She also remained totally non-judgmental.

When I refused to work, she helped me feel understood and see what was really going on. When I felt icky about a choice that I made or an action that I took, she taught me to show myself compassion whilst learning to be better next time. Every time I judged and shamed myself for not being perfect, she reminded me that I was, regardless of anything, because what I was experiencing was simply a measure of my evolution, not my fear.

Through our relationship, I learnt more about who I was and who I could become—not because she told me but because she gave me the courage to tell myself. I learnt that I could do whatever the fuck I wanted, whenever the fuck I wanted, and it would always be perfect. No judgment, no shame, no labels, no Separation. Just life.

That was 5D; not the fact that Liz could speak to Angels, not the fact that we could meditate together, and not even the work itself. It was the fact that we could laugh about our nail color, joke about our road rage, gossip about the night before, and we could do Pilates (her) and lay on the ground pretending to do Pilates (me) knowing that it was all divine.

This isn't a manifesto on how great Liz is, nor is it about finding one person. Rather, it's about who we become as a result of our relationships and who we become after that. It's about what we can create with others once we know ourselves. That's where it gets really yummy, and that's what we've been searching for all along. But it also doesn't have to be about relationships with others. It can be our relationships with our work, our passions, or the ways we express ourselves sartorially. How we shine our light is perfect for us because, ultimately, it's about our relationship with ourselves and how we express it.

It wasn't just my relationship with Liz that was divine because we were talking about the Divine a lot. It was every friend who triggered me, laughed with me, got tipsy with me, and passed me a tissue; it was every person who walked into my life and walked out of it—and sometimes walked back in again. It was my sister, my mother, my father, and my family who may not have been related to me but felt like home in some way. It was the best friend who showed me the door of that dance class, the one who was so compassionate I could finally understand what that meant, and the one who encouraged me to just act in whatever way felt right to me.

They all taught me what a relationship was. They all taught me what I wanted my relationships to look like. Ultimately, they all taught me more about who I was and what I stood for. That's spirituality to me, and that's the best way that I can experience the Divine in action.

That Thing You Do

According to my mother, I started singing when I was nine months old. I was in the car (during a particularly long drive), and I started singing a nursery rhyme pitch perfect. Now, my mother has been known to exaggerate all her children's abilities, but either way, it makes for a great start to a chapter.

From the second I could walk, I walked out in front of my family to perform for them. Every Christmas, birthday, and family gathering, and for no particular reason, I could be found standing in a circle of people, singing my heart out. By two, I was the head fairy with a solo in school; by nine, I was in one-on-one singing lessons; by ten, I was singing in front of over 100 people; and by twelve, it was part of my identity.

I would be trotted out at friend's houses to sing for their families, I would be trotted out at charity events, and I would be trotted out at competitions. I made up songs that are still family anthems, I made up dances to accompany them, and I would perform to millions from my bedroom with a hairbrush as a microphone—which got so annoying that my family would beg me to just shut up.

When I sang, I could not only convey emotion but also allow other people to connect to theirs. My voice was powerful, and when I gave it my all, it could fill a room easily (which makes more sense why my family asked me to stop singing all the time). But I was also taught that taking up space was not okay and what made us unique made us different. So the older I got, the quieter my voice became, until I stopped singing completely.

I used to say that it was because when I went to university and hanging out in the singing hall wasn't going to get me laid (although not hanging out in the singing hall didn't get me laid, either). I argued singing wasn't a career but a hobby, and following the "right" path and having the "right" job was a lot safer. But I stopped singing because even though I loved it, I lost the joy that underpinned it. So, instead of trying to find the light within, I decided to try to find something external to light me up in its place.

It wasn't just singing that fell foul to this game. I shelved everything about me that I was good at, which didn't have a clear use. Whether it was being able to figure out how to use random bits of software because I wanted to create something (people would tell me to pursue a career in video editing), being able to connect with others (people would tell me to consider a career in PR), being able to take big ideas and seeing the core of the issue (people would tell me to explore a career as a psychologist), or being able to figure out a problem and find a simple solution (people would tell me to think about a career in law; I followed that one to my detriment).

Every talent or skill that I had that came easily to me and that brought me joy was pushed to the side. Unless they could be turned into a ragingly successful business, there wasn't any point. And even then there were people out there who were better than me at it, so I shouldn't bother in the first place.

In the scheme of things, our human life appears fairly inconsequential. We are part of a huge solar system, which is part of a huge galaxy within an even bigger universe. There are billions of people on Earth, and for every story about heartbreak or triumph, there are many who have similar stories that outshine ours. We are consistently told there is nothing special about our experiences, and that is meant to shrink our problems into nothing as well. But that's perpetuating the problem. We pretend we feel great whilst feeling pretty Shitty and looking at other people worse off than us (the only way to feel bigger is if someone else is smaller—isn't that the theory of relativity?).

We believe that it is only when we make money, achieve stability, or gain recognition for our talents that they have value. We believe we are so small and inconsequential that we cannot believe how powerful we are. And we don't believe in our experience of life, so we can't make it matter to us. However, we hold all the answers that we desperately seek from other people. Our souls have been leaving us breadcrumbs back to our joy from the second we came into body. We just can't see it when we allow Separation to cloud our view. So, even if we tell ourselves we don't know where to begin making our lives better, there is a part of us that does.

I couldn't find an upside to my life when I was cutting all the joy out of it (except for sex, maybe… but even then, I would still ask myself, "Was it worth it?"). But the key to my healing and empowerment wasn't about going on a cosmic scavenger hunt, it was to figure out why I was here. All those talents that I enjoyed were pointing the way, and in the moments where I engaged in joy, I made them count. I also created something far bigger than me, which became a container of that joy to share with others.

Everything that came easily to me was all the things that I needed to create Karma's My Bitch. It was the same for Liz. Together, we had everything we needed, through our talents and skills, to bring a whole body of work with all the trimmings through—and then to life—and it all came from inside of us. We were taking our light and allowing it to be seen by the world. I thought it was freaky, but looking back, it was fate.

I knew why I was here. I didn't want anyone to spend another second in Separation, let alone an afternoon, and I definitely didn't want anyone to experience karma if they didn't have to. And with this work, I stand a chance of doing that. With our light, we created tools for others to shine theirs too—so that, hopefully, one day, their children and grandchildren won't need karma to know their power.

When I stopped trying to commodify my joy, I took the small me, who had kept quiet because she didn't want to fill up the room, and helped her become the largest version of herself. I used my voice in every way I could, and I not only healed my Shit but found a way for others to do the same. Then, one day, I found myself singing in the shower again, I found myself singing in the car, and I found myself singing on Spotify.

Starman
Liz

Imagine being an only child with no one to play with but having the ability to create whatever we desire. Now, I don't mean creating humans and the whole Creation story about Adam, a rib, and boom, there's Eve. Rather, picture a void and then life existing within that void—life, not in human form, but the potential of what it can be outside of just cellular matter. It is complete and total potential.

Just imagine what could be done with all that potential creation. Imagine how, beyond universes and galaxies, there is life in a variety of forms that exist, perhaps not as flesh and blood. Consider for a moment, if we have the power to create something from the void as an only child, how we might be able to experience more than a single-player game. Imagine being able to become different players with distinct forms of thinking, logic, and reactions to play the game and make it challenging. (Anyone who has tried to play a two-person game by themselves will understand that what makes it difficult to enjoy is you will always be able to anticipate the next move making it not challenging and downright boring.) But to accomplish this means having to spread out a bit because creation needs space to exist, which, in turn, requires destruction to make that space. That space could be an entire world devoted entirely to life. Then, extend that image out to something more far-reaching and even vaster than you have conceived before—there are more places and spaces for creation to just be.

To experience creation of any kind requires the possibility for that creation to thrive by providing a place for it to be nurtured and to be aware of its existence. Otherwise, how would it know it exists? (Kind of like when a tree falls in a forest, does it make a sound?) And, for some, it may not be enough to think ourselves into existence (Descartes' *Cogito, ergo sum*: I think, therefore I am). It might be that the only way to really "know" is to live through each of our bodies (emotional, physical, mental, and spiritual) to fully express our being. Since creation is dynamic, the ideal way to play in creation is often to be dynamic.

But creation is only dynamic because it is a living, breathing organism. It is life force in physical form. Like all creation, it bears an imprint of whatever created it, much like children to their parents. Yet, no one is an exact replica of their creator. It wouldn't be very interesting to have everything as the exact same make or model. Having to face ourselves in the mirror every morning becomes boring and *quotidien*, so why would anyone want to stare at a hundred or more versions of the same person? It helps to be unique enough to distinguish one from the other while acknowledging the same divinity underneath, a bit like cosmic dress-up. This is how Otherness began.

Now, consider for a moment what Otherness looks like in Separation. For a soul to come into 3D consciousness, it has to regard its Otherness as something wholly and entirely separate from itself. Accordingly, the soul is regarded not as an extension of the Divine but as an entirely different being.

This is why free will became necessary. Since Source cannot exist in Separation, souls needed complete and full agency to operate in 3D as they would not have a complete divine connection. Thus, when a soul had to regard itself, it did so without the light of the Divine and with the consciousness of Separation. So, its Otherness is not merely an attribute or trait; it became something to be judged and reconciled with this new consciousness. How shockingly painful that could be, but also how incredibly liberating and fascinating an experience—like jumping out of an airplane without a parachute but expecting to land safely.

Yet, we may look at history and ask ourselves, "Would anyone really 'choose' this life if it is so painful and exposes us to all sorts of difficult challenges and the sordid experiences that life on Earth brings? But like any adrenaline junkie or someone who seeks adventure, the answer any soul would give would be, "Hell yes."

First of all, because it can, knowing full well that life is really temporary and not nearly for as long as human time would have us believe since time is not linear. Second, to have the fully loaded experience of the entire consciousness spectrum that is allowed on

Earth, including Separation to the fullest degree. As we've witnessed through our karma, there are infinite ways we can experience Separation, and humans are quite creative about it all. It's just one roller coaster after another, and if we really need a boost in evolution, Earth is the perfect place for a soul to get a Ph.D. in consciousness raising.

Since consciousness is the complete and utter knowing that resides within our core, sometimes we need a few experiences or several lifetimes to reach that knowing and for it to penetrate our different bodies. Life on Earth offers a host of experiences for eager virgins and Separation experts alike. While it may seem illogical to choose something unpleasant time and again, it becomes more understandable when we understand that it serves a greater purpose.

Besides, life in Separation was Bangkok for the soul's growth. Thanks to the rules of polarity, there are always the good, the highs, and the beauty interspersed throughout our lifetimes that shape our consciousness, giving space to experience love, joy, pleasure, and hope. These are also the things souls come to Earth for. The 3D spectrum of Separation, along with the free will to do whatever the fuck they want, gives them such rich opportunities no other place could offer (go to Bangkok, and you'll know what I mean).

Souls embarking on this consciousness quest do so knowing full well they'll be forced to forget the Divine just enough to make the experience real—a bit like virtual reality. We need to be immersed enough to make it real to the senses, but a part of us is always aware that we're not really in the story. The issue arises when life in Separation makes us forget our purpose entirely because we've forgotten who we are. We can end up becoming so immersed in the experience that we forget the Divine more and more. It could be that there were too many lifetimes in the dark, too many existences that involved fear or the absence of light. When we don't have enough light, it is easy to lose our way.

The fear we hold in 3D blocks us from seeing the larger picture and our place in it, which is merely to play out a life of our choosing. We chose to try out Separation to understand what disempowerment is like to come into our power, a bit like children coming into adulthood. But the longer we remained disempowered, the more we began to play out more lifetimes and collective stories around it until it became normalized. For many souls who have had numerous lifetimes on Earth, they have not been able to emerge from 3D precisely because of how embedded their consciousness is in Separation. They are the ones who currently struggle with the leap into 5D and steadfastly hold on to 3D. It is really all they have ever known.

This has been the greatest challenge behind the human experiment. On the one hand, it is creation at its finest because it has developed a consciousness and means to exercise the most divine power of all—to create and destroy. Yet, life in Separation means many souls have become lost to the destructive forces that humanity has unleashed. To be fair, it's merely the result of creativity gone awry, but it has compelled so many souls to come and join the consciousness-raising effort.

These souls on a mission, Aliens, and purpose-filled souls are here to help course-correct. Humanity is far too important to the whole fabric of our existence to allow it to wipe itself out with its own foibles and messes, which is at risk of happening because of Separation. But now that Separation can cease to be due to our rising consciousness, so too can the disastrous messes humankind is so skilled at making. In its place, a new consciousness can emerge that allows everyone to harness the power that enables them to direct their lives from that place of Oneness and harmony.

Just Like Heaven

Karma is the pathway to wholeness, from 3D to 5D, or Separation to Oneness. Karma effectively enlists free will to create the illusion that we are free enough to choose a different illusion. This illusion tells us that we are so free that we have complete and total agency over our lives (which we do, just not in 3D), thus muting our ego enough to move out of the chokehold it has over us. It allows us to believe our life is finally manageable, that everything is possible, and that we are finally in control. It brings us to a place where we can touch, experience, or feel the Divine in our lives simply because we feel in charge. Life might finally feel it belongs to us, that our luck has changed, and that the worst is behind us. But if we haven't fully resolved our core fear that we are not *good enough*, karma will ensure we face it, one way or another. No amount of free will can stop it.

It may seem unfair. If we don't have a lot of ego and don't carry enough fear, that *should* be enough for us to live in peace. Free will alone *should* be enough to get us through this lifetime. True, except this lifetime is ruled by the transition into Oneness, which means free will can no longer be in service to humanity the way it was before. Free will is the energy that enables 3D to exist by essentially creating the illusion that we are separate from the Divine. If we are to move from 3D to 5D, we cannot maintain any illusion that we are separate from the Divine, or that would defeat the whole purpose of the entire exercise.

While releasing ourselves from Separation might feel like the chore of a lifetime, it merely begins with understanding that relinquishing the need for free will doesn't cut us off from our will but allows that will to expand into something greater. All that we need to do are the following three things:

1. Be a badass.

Life will continue to show us that the answer to any of our issues cannot come from anyone but ourselves. Of course, it may help to have a sounding board. It would likely serve us to have a friend or mentor to help us work through our Shit. We are not meant to go into Oneness alone. However, the dependence on the idea that someone else will provide the solution or answer or save us is precisely what keeps us in our victimhood. We may not have it all figured out from the get-go, but fuck if we're not some of the most creative, clever creatures in body at the moment. And until we believe that we got this, we don't have anything. So be the badass who keeps pivoting, doesn't give up, and doesn't take no for an answer.

2. Be generous.

We've forgotten how to give. The result is that we have lost a sense of connection and community, which has pulled us farther apart from one another. While this happened in part to allow us to come into our individual power, it has hampered our evolution because we've become energetic hoarders, reserving all of our power and peace for ourselves and no one else. But if we only sit back and witness the destruction of our old world, without contributing our gifts and talents to the rebuilding, then we are no better off than when we started. The key is to remember that we are in this together, like it or not. 5D is a collective effort, not an individual one.

3. Be a little bit crazy.

Oneness is not about planning or knowing what is next. When we are at One with ourselves, we are at One with our path, which unfolds as we walk and dance along it. We can know if we are still operating from free will because we will look to guideposts while plotting out our course. When we are operating from divine will, we won't need guideposts since everything is in line with our fate. It may not make sense to everyone else, but if our hearts beam and want to explode from our chests when we are living the life we determine, then it's safe to say we're doing what we want. That is divine will, and that is freedom.

Free will itself is merely one of many divine energies that were gifted to us to make the most of a life in Separation where we could not exist fully in our divine power. But when we can recognize and source that divine power from within, we can fully actualize the spiritual part of ourselves. It's an opportunity we've never had before because it isn't possible when Separation is present. But when we are whole and Divine, our souls come alive again, and that is when things get interesting.

Love Is A Beautiful Thing
Rhea

When we make any choice that feels right, we allow our light to fill our worlds. We're turning up as ourselves and facilitating the possibility that we can have everything we want—which is simply to be ourselves and for it to work out in our favor. But even though we cannot always see how it will work out in our favor; it doesn't matter.

I could have justified my life and made excuses for my unhappiness. I could have settled in relationships where only half of me was present whilst the other half was cowering in the corner or hidden under the bed. I could have figured that part out and focused on the relationships between two people until the day that I died, and it probably would have been *better enough*. But it wouldn't have been enough, despite how much I told myself otherwise.

I also never would have understood why relationships mattered so much to me. I only would have evidenced how to make them that little bit better. However, in making choice after choice that felt aligned with me (despite the seemingly crazy nature of those choices), I saw where my understanding of relationships could take me. I saw what

I was capable of, and I allowed my understanding of Love to expand with me.

Love isn't just something that is shared between two people, a family, or even with our work or passions. It's how we push ourselves out of who we knew ourselves to be and into a world where we can achieve everything we desire. It's how we embody our power to the point that we are untouchable. But that isn't because we don't need anyone else or because our internal world is the only one that matters. We don't want to be shining our light into a black hole until we're so tired that we quit. In shining that light, we connect to the higher power that we all have within us that says we can keep experimenting, playing, learning, and growing in a way that makes sense to us—even if we can't see where we're going. That's how people who match that light and amplify it can walk beside us and create that world with us.

The more Love we hold, the more Love is reflected back in experiences and joy. For me to be the best version of myself, I also had to be in Love. I had to enjoy my life and everything that came with it (which often included other joyful people). It wasn't about making the best of a bad situation and accepting it, nor was it about #gratitude. It was accepting that I had all the answers and always did.

That's the secret we've alluded to in these books and the one I get the pleasure of doing a big reveal for (it's not a secret at all, and some of you may have already guessed it, but my job is to bang people over the head, so here we go). Every choice we make when we follow our hearts comes back to who we are, and every choice we make when we know who we are is us expressing that person. All we are doing when shining that light through trust, hope, faith, and knowing is acknowledging how divine we can be. It's us, embodying our higher self, even for a moment, and changing the trajectory of our lives. It allows us to open our eyes to who we really are and the knowledge that we've always been divine.

Love Story

Love is shining our light unapologetically for everyone to see through our words, actions, and our being. It isn't just one person who brings out our Love, it comes through us every time we engage in anything that brings us joy, and it's through Love that we can change our perspective.

That's the beauty of Love and why relationships are so important, especially the ones we have with ourselves. It isn't about finding a body to share a cold night, a devoted partner, a passion-fueled job, or even a sacred connection to the All. It's about all of it and more. Love fortifies our wisdom so that we can light the path that leads us to happiness.

In following my light, I found more than just myself. I found a fuller, more expanded self that could do a whole lot more than I could have foreseen. It may have seemed like I was only making small decisions, but when I saw how those decisions weaved together, I understood that every step led me to the right place at the right time. Every time. In listening to myself and acting accordingly, I became present in the relationships I had once longed for, the work that I never believed I could create, and the courage to see it all through.

Every relationship I put my heart into helped me see my light in a different hue. I saw that I had the power to change my circumstances for the better, simply by being myself rather than embodying the patterns I developed as a result of my misguided beliefs. In approaching my relationships, work, and physical body from a different, more expanded place, I operated harmoniously. As a result, new opportunities arose in the place of old problems that no longer applied.

This isn't because I have some secret practice that allows me to make the most of life. It also isn't because I have access to Guidance, a work wife who puts up with my (often) self-centered approach to life, or even a job that allows me to navel gaze until I get bored of my own belly button. It's simply because I had the faith to reconnect to myself and trust my life to unfold. In doing so, I saw the best part—that I was right all along. It really was all about Love.

Everyone in this world is capable of realizing their own happiness, which means that everyone can choose what that looks like for themselves. As scary as that may be, it's also fucking beautiful and one of the most liberating things I've ever learnt. Not only does it allow us to serve ourselves to fill our lives with light, but it also allows that light to serve others.

As a reformed people pleaser, understanding that others were just as responsible for their lives as I was for mine was one of the perspectives that changed everything. I treated them with the same respect I showed myself, and I allowed them to express their desires in the same way that I expressed mine. I also started to listen (which, for anyone who knows me, was kind of a big deal).

It allowed the relationships, whatever they were, to be free; I could finally comprehend that we were all powerful—not just me, and not just them. This added a beautiful dynamic to every interaction I had because that freedom allowed the interaction to live up to its potential rather than wither under the combined weight of our expectations.

When Liz talks about the I/Thou dynamic, I believe that is what she means. That isn't just nice; to me, it's fucking spiritual. It allows us to have faith in ourselves, but it also allows us to have faith in one another. Faith stops being something that's experienced alone and becomes something that can be shared. Not because you lend it to another person or prove it, but because when you have faith in yourself, you can recognize it in another and create something in the physical world.

This may sound confusing, but let me explain it in the context of Liz and I. Even when I wanted to quit, even when things got dicey, and even when she pissed me off by giving Yoda-like answers to very simple questions, I kept going. I kept showing up because I wanted to. I was just as annoying. I made everything about me, I barely let her get a word in, and I was hellbent on proving that spirituality was crap whilst knowing somewhere deep inside that it wasn't. But she showed up, too. We both kept showing up for each other, for work, and for our friendship—surprising each other in the process.

This new world doesn't have to be spiritual, or at least not in the way we think it needs to be, when words like 5D, Oneness, and harmony get thrown into the mix. It just needs to be an expression of our light, whatever the hue and wherever it shines. That doesn't start from someone outside of us, nor is it offered by some otherworldly being that bestows our dreams upon us. We are the only ones who know what our dreams are, which means we are the only ones who can make them come true.

That's the world we are here to live in, and that's what we came for—not to struggle and suffer until we die or to follow someone else's rules. It's to be our unique selves, as best as we can be, and enjoy what happens next. That's why we have to put our hearts into our worlds, relationships, and lives. It's how we can make something meaningful out of our post-karmic reality.

Our power is the gift that spirituality leaves us with. It's the gift that keeps on giving because we keep on giving, too—until no one ever has to make karma their bitch again because their divinity is a given. In giving ourselves the chance to know what is best for us, act in our best interest, and share that best self with others, we get all of that back and more. Love really does get us there; all we have to do is follow it and allow others to come for the ride. That's when the fun can really start.

The Edge Of Heaven
Liz

2012 heralded the new age of consciousness. We've had a variety of peaks and moments throughout our history, but as far as critical years go, it was one of the biggest ones we'd had since 1988 and the harmonic conversion of Earth's vibration. This is when Earth's vibration was raised to such a degree that no being, entity, or thing below 3D energy could enter.

2012 was the year to mark the beginning of the beginning. While it's funny to assume we started something new while recognizing we were bringing another age to a close, we have been in a long cycle of beginnings and endings. It's at that time the spirals of the old age and the new age came close to each other, long enough for us to see how far we've come and how much further we have to go.

While perhaps 2012 had been predicted by some ancient civilization, its significance wasn't so much about 2012 but about who we'd be as a civilization once we reached it. Were we either advanced enough in our consciousness to bring Earth and her inhabitants into the Age of Harmony, or were we going to persist in our limiting beliefs that would ensure the end of humanity's potential? To answer this, we needed to be far enough along in our consciousness and technology, whereby one could assist the other to elevate the human experience and free it from its enslavement to the 3D tentpoles.

This was the critical question faced in 2012: have we collectively evolved enough to bring forth a new age without fully destroying the old one first?

Frankly, the answer was negative. Yet, we don't destroy merely because we're failing at something, because there's still enough consciousness to keep us afloat. We can see how much further we can go and keep going; ultimately, we either render ourselves obsolete or grow. Those are our two options in the world of Separation.

We have been living in Shitty scenarios since we were born. Whether within our own family structures or on a global scale, we are continually confronted by Separation—not to cower and surrender and just accept it for what it is but to accept that it isn't how it has to be. If we can will one world into existence, we can certainly will a new one in its place. But it's only possible if we can access our will and put it into practice. Karma gives us that space to do it from the micro to the macro scale, so if we can change one Shitty thing about our lives, then we can have the faith to change one Shitty thing about the world.

Any meaningful impact we have begins when we listen to ourselves and recognize our ability to create something entirely different. This is displayed not by our intolerance for old 3D systems but by our desire to create a new one—one that is based on wholeness and Oneness, not Separation and polarity.

That we couldn't foresee what's to come or even a minute of the end of Separation speaks to how embedded we've become in 3D. We were caught with our pants down. We were so busy making the best of it that we didn't see how Separation bested us and that we were too unconscious and complacent to see it coming. Releasing ourselves requires embracing what freedom really means to us, which isn't easy. It's actually quite the opposite because we don't know what that looks like. We've never experienced a lifetime of complete and utter freedom. It's overwhelming because we've always had someone—from parents to the government or some religious figure—control our movements, define our values, and give us purpose.

As humans, we consistently ensure our own self-destruction time and again. Just look at our recent history (say, the past twenty years). Whenever we are presented with opportunities for peace, we seek to divide. Despite promises for a new world in a new age, we feed upon recycled events caused by the same hatred, intolerance, and vitriol that find their way back into our realities, since nothing ever got healed.

Nothing can ever be healed completely in Separation. All we do is fit a few disparate pieces of our karmic puzzle together before starting over in a new life. Over and over, same hamster wheel, new challenges to heal those other parts that didn't get tended to in the previous life—and then boom, time to try again.

But finally. FINALLY. This. Is. It. How do we know this is it? Because I say so? Because Rhea says so? Because the Guides say so? Because God says so?

No, not at all. No one gets to declare when except those of us who are in body. Humanity gets an upgrade when our consciousness does. What makes this lifetime different from all other lifetimes is simply one thing: our consciousness has expanded to the point that we can live, breathe, and taste this thing called Oneness. It's not some far-off ideal anymore, nor is it some tripping hippy's dreamed-up notion of peace and love. This got real because our growing awareness made it real. We are coming to comprehend that our reality is shaped by us because it's an extension of our consciousness. As a result, anything that happens in our reality comes from our role in it. So, if we want a better reality, we have to be the ones who make it better.

That's not karma, that's fate, and 5D consciousness is fated. It is written. There is absolutely no chance that it's not. It's not a cosmic joke, nor is it some myth created by some ancient civilization. Rather, it's a new era that's meant to usher in new principles and values by which the future of humankind can live and thrive.

Integrity and compassion form the foundation for 5D Oneness consciousness. Without it, we remain in 3D. Integrity and compassion are the roots of the I/Thou relationship: "I recognize the light within You and live to express the light within Me." This fundamental viewpoint allows us to treat others with compassion, and when we hold others in compassion, we cannot hold them in a space of judgment.

When we operate from our divine power, "I did it for you" takes on a whole new meaning because we are moving I/You to I/Thou. For as much as I do for you, I do for myself. Not in a 50/50, give-and-take kind of way; rather, I live from an expanded place of purpose, consciousness, and integrity, so I have the capacity to see you as I see myself. To see that and how we are connected means I can hold space for it All.

New Age loves a good label because that's what Separation requires for us to quantify or understand. Yet, no one is served when we label one another. Whether they go by indigo, rainbow, crystal, or their generational alphabet, all that matters is that anyone in body today is here for this consciousness shift, whether or not their auras or spiritual DNA says so. That's the goal of this entire consciousness game: to stop focusing on each other's differences and instead see our divine connection to everyone.

To understand why certain souls hold so much significance in our New Age community, we have to examine our propensity for hero or savior worship—those who "come down" from the heavens to save us poor cursed beings. Except they were never going to save humanity until humanity could help itself. Otherwise, any efforts would be lost by the next generation and keep us locked in our perpetual karmic cycles, never to end Separation.

Our ever-growing consciousness, coupled with the support from our Guides, helps make this lifetime different from every other. With every passing year, we are making strides to see how this world can be different; and with every new generation coming in, our tolerance for Separation lowers. But it's precisely because we've tolerated it for so much of our current lifetimes and continue to foist on younger generations that it's taking time to change, time that many of us feel we lack.

Yet, as Rhea says, time isn't our enemy, not if we can exist outside of it and not be tethered to the warped version of it in 3D. When we assimilate to our own time, as in live according to what works or suits us best, we can untangle ourselves from Separation and make choices that express our fate.

This may seem nearly impossible, given how our world is set up. Day turns into night, work hours are shoved into neat compartments with appropriate break times, and we are allotted a certain number of days off if we're lucky enough to not have to think about work, which is rare since so much of what we do revolves around what we need to do to survive as opposed to living in pursuit of Love. We don't have to lose ourselves in the process, we just have to be willing to lose the things that get in the way, which is effectively the fear that tells us we'll lose it all. But it doesn't have to be that way. We can get more. More Love, more fun, and more life to live—it's all there for the taking. We just have to show up and give it our best shot.

What seals Oneness (the understanding that we are all One, which upholds harmony, peace, and compassion) in our personal reality is a whole, healed heart. If we haven't managed to heal it through our karmic story, we have to go about it a different way: through Time, though not in the sense that "time heals all wounds" by putting space between ourselves and the point of trauma but rather Time when viewed through the lens of our divinity, that is, Attunement. When we are in a state of Attunement, every bit of our being is attuned to the Divine. This includes not only our four main bodies (physical, emotional, mental, and spiritual) but every ounce of our consciousness, without a fragment left in Separation.

Often, we can live from at least one of these bodies. Each book in this karmic series has addressed them, and we've shown how to build from individual power—whether you are living with purpose or living in Love—to divine power. In other words, to own our divinity is knowing we are capable and wholly aligned with something more than our karmic fates and also have a larger capacity to hold more than we thought.

Most cannot speak to this. Frankly, complete removal from the physical world was pretty much the only way to achieve happiness in 3D Separation, which is why it eluded everyone. However, as we stand on the precipice of 5D, uncertain of what lies before us, there is the inkling that happiness is finally possible, and we can wake up day after day without the highs and lows that have marked many of our lives. Rather, have the steady emotional baseline feeling assured that, despite what is happening in our external world, our internal one is safe and sound.

While it may sound like peace, the difference between happiness and peace is that the former is us in our most divine space in all we are, think, do, and say, whereas the latter is merely a sense that whatever we are, do, think, and say is enough at that point in time.

The differences are ultimately minor but important because happiness is truly a part of our fate. That means whatever we do, so long as it is in line with our fate, we create our own happiness. And happiness is not something we can experience while we are in the midst of our karma. Ever. Karma is not, nor was it ever, part of our fate. It was merely intended to get us to burn out everything that would keep us from realizing our fate, which was never to suffer or live a life of mediocrity until we died. That's part of karma's magic. It forces us to contend with all our demons, from the inside out, until we can transcend all our Shit and move into the larger fabric of our fate.

Happiness is the sum total of our fate. It is the intersection where all the roads meet and brings us exactly where we are meant to be. We know exactly when we reach that point because we do not look to what's ahead, nor do we regard what we've left behind. At this juncture, some internal voice (that is, our higher self) tells us, "This is it," and we don't doubt it for a minute.

We came into this lifetime at this specific time to hold the space for 5D consciousness to come into this Earth plane. So, when we are out of our karmic stories and embarking on the broader path of our fate, we are doing so with the full knowledge that we're here for something, even if we may not know everything. But because we do not have all the details, we're forced to operate from faith—faith that we'll reach our intended destination, however it happens, and faith that we are powerful enough to take on any of the challenges that arise along the way.

Our souls will guide us to our purpose. When we've divested ourselves of enough of our fears, karma, and ego, we can listen to those inklings of desire that show up more and more. The more tuned in to our desires we become, the more we recognize how they fit into our purpose; and the more we give ourselves permission to follow what brings us joy, the more freedom we give ourselves.

Once we have that clarity, everything falls in line, and we no longer have to fight for our freedom. It becomes a given. We've merely been living our story backwards rather than as empowered beings who know how to be happy and fulfilled. Not only are we realizing that we have the power to make it better, but there are enough of us to see it come to fruition. That's what the 2012 prophecy was all about—the gods walking among us. We are those gods who walk the Earth. Each one of us who can grasp our truest, fullest divinity is the Divine in body.

This demands one thing of us: to venture into the unknown because it is in the unknown where all the potential and magic lies. Where there's freedom, happiness, and power, the Divine is at the heart of it all, and when the Divine is present, everything is possible. First, we learn to Love, then we learn to share that Love, and then we learn to apply that Love to everything we do. That's how we make magic.

About KMB

Rhea always had a strong desire to seek justice. Whether it was through learning about law or working on the team that criminalized coercive control, she never stopped trying to help others. It wasn't until after a few life hiccups that she understood the most effective way to help others was to transform her life first. A podcast and several books about karma, magic, and following your heart later, she figured out how to create her own happiness and how to teach others to do the same.

With nearly twenty years' experience as a spiritual advisor to clients around the world, Liz is a medium and Soul Memory Discovery facilitator, who also writes steamy novels under the pen name Vivian Winslow. Her work taught her that despite our surface differences, people are driven by two essential things: a need for love and a desire to find meaning.

Together they created Karma Magic Bliss (or KMB for short) to offer all the tools and information to allow people to realize the lives they desire. This includes free resources (the podcast Karma's My Bitch) as well as in-depth explanations (the books) and practical learning material. To find out more about KMB and what's coming, you can visit www.wearekmb.com or drop a line through @karmamagicbliss on all social platforms.

Acknowledgments

Usually in these books, both Liz and I write the acknowledgements together. But when we finished the draft for *A Karmic Adventure*, it became clear to us that for this, the final book in this series, that honor was mine.

Like so many things in my karmic journey, this wasn't something I expected. I was too focused on finishing everything, getting to the next series, and seeing what life could be without the weight of anything karmic resting on my shoulders. I didn't think that the acknowledgements could be significant. I also didn't think we had anyone left to thank (four books in a series will do that). But when I understood why I had to write these, I also understood what I had to acknowledge because this isn't just a simple thank you to the people who helped us get this book through the final stages of completion. It is the acknowledgement of six years of work—both professionally and personally—that has culminated in this final exercise.

For a long time, I wasn't proud of the person who walked through Liz's door in 2018. I was lost, confused, angry, and skeptical. As much as I wanted more for my life, I also didn't think it was possible. I hoped that Liz would help me assuage my hopelessness, but I didn't think she could do it. In fact, I hesitated at every juncture when it came to this work, and even though I eventually said yes to it all, it wasn't always an easy choice. I may have wanted to believe that my life could get better, but I couldn't be sure that the work would actually work.

I don't need to go through what happened to me. My story is on the pages of every one of our books (hopefully, Liz's chapters broke it up a bit). But I do need to acknowledge that as much as I doubted that my fate would lead me to my redemption, it did. That is why I am now totally proud of who I was. If it wasn't for her, I wouldn't be where I am today. This work has given me so much more than an author credit, it has given me back my life. I know now, without a shadow of a doubt, that it works. I am living the dreams that I shelved for too long, as well as others that I didn't see coming but are so perfect for me that I should have thought of them first.

But I didn't do it alone. I may be in the driver's seat of my life, but I was given the right directions. Liz showed more faith in me than I often showed myself. She listened to me cry, scream, bitch, and laugh. She held my hand when things got dark, and she helped me find more light. She pushed me to be a better version of myself at every juncture and reminded me that only I could know what was best for myself. She graciously shared her experience at every turn and answered every question, no matter how banal or how many times I'd already asked. I came into this work looking for partnership, and I found it in more ways than I ever could have envisaged.

ACKNOWLEDGMENTS

That is what this work gives us: more of what we want and better than we could have imagined. We don't need to live with karma forever; my story attests to that. It doesn't give us a way to feel relief or even mildly satisfied. It allows who we are to be expressed in a multitude of ways—so that everywhere we look is another example of how great life is. It is a gift that I wanted to give back more times than I can count, but now I am so grateful it didn't have a favorable return policy. A life without karma is a life well worth every second that preceded it.

To me, these books have been about connection—connecting to our larger selves, connecting to other people, and connecting the dots. They've been a manual of sorts to creating a joyful life and finding real happiness. But there was a time when I didn't want to connect to anything. I wasn't always the easiest friend, the greatest date, or even an interesting dinner companion. However, the people in my life have loved me regardless and have been there for me in ways that sometimes I wasn't sure I deserved. I know that Liz will explain that's the nature of soul contracts, but that doesn't negate how special they are. I often look at the people who surround me and feel deeply grateful that I get the chance to love them back. Contracts or not, if that's not an indication of the Divine at work, I don't know what is.

Which brings me to Guidance. I know, fucking strange to be thanking them, but they are the third partner in our merry trio. They pushed us, kept us on track, had our backs, and made this whole journey a lot more interesting. They enjoyed their "big reveals," and they managed us even when we didn't think we needed it. Working with them remains a huge privilege that we do not, nor cannot, take for granted.

It's easy to take this life for granted and get caught up in the humdrum of our days without ever acknowledging the magic that surrounds us. But there's magic everywhere, even if we can't always see it. That's why our next series is about magic and what happens when we finally realize our power. It's going to be a different kind of adventure but until then, if you have any questions about our work, please get in touch through our socials (@karmamagicbliss on all platforms) or through our website: www.wearekmb.com.

Printed in Great Britain
by Amazon